# Praise for *The Kitchen C...*

"Writing with downright elegance that always delivers the ...
phrase or insight, Seton explores the kitchen's meaning for women ...
the center of the home—the place where friends gather to drink coffee
and share secrets....Seton's memories of her mother's slow death from
cancer and the stillbirth of her own first child are poignant but never
depressing because she conveys such a palpable sense of life as a process,
of experiences that...always enrich the soul."       —Amazon.com

"By page three I was at the cash register and ten minutes later, home in
my favorite easy chair....I couldn't bear the thought of finishing this
book so quickly. But I couldn't bear to stay away from author Nora
Seton and the other women who make up *The Kitchen Congregation*."
                      —*The Capital Times* (Madison, Wisconsin)

"Recipes and secrets provide the flavors that make the extraordinary
out of the ordinary. Friends and mentors all, the women who make up
this kitchen congregation are a group well worth meeting, and well
worth honoring for what they have to teach."       —*Booklist*

"Seton here moves us through time to various kitchens she's enjoyed
with special friends and family members and embellishes reminiscences
with cherished recipes that revive the spirit....Seton's warm, fluid
prose is woven together beautifully."       —*Library Journal*

"Seton portrays the women and their kitchen spaces with the unique
flavor of their personal styles and lives. The reader feels that she/he has
been in each home, smelling specialties bubbling or baking away, and
even comes away with a homey recipe or two. Seton successfully serves
up the kitchen as a female metaphor, equally compassionate for those
who have embraced the role(s) and those who have resisted being tied
to the stove."       —*The Bloomsbury Review*

# The Kitchen Congregation

## Nora Seton

Picador USA

New York

This book is for Chuck.

Picador® is a U.S. registered trademark and is used by St. Martin's Press under license from Pan Books Limited.

For information on Picador USA Reading Group Guides, as well as ordering, please contact the Trade Marketing department at St. Martin's Press.
Phone: 1-800-221-7945 extension 763
Fax: 212-677-7456
E-mail: trademarketing@stmartins.com

Note to the Reader:
Names have been changed to protect privacies.

Permissions: "A Story and a Song," by A. K. Ramanujan, in *A Flowering Tree and Other Oral Tales from India*, edited and translated by Dundes Blackbur, copyright © 1996 by The Regents of the University of California. Reprinted in modified form by permission of the University of California Press.

Designed by Michelle McMillian

Library of Congress Cataloging-in-Publication Data

Seton, Nora Janssen.
    The kitchen congregation : a daughter's story of wives and women friends / Nora Seton.
        p. cm.
    ISBN 0-312-24210-7 (hc)
    ISBN 0-312-26348-1 (pbk)
    1. Seton, Cynthia Propper—Family. 2. Novelists, American—20th century—Family relationships. 3. Mothers—Death—Psychological aspects. 4. Mothers and daughters—United States. 5. Women—United States—Biography. 6. Seton, Nora Janssen—Family.
    7. Motherhood. 8. Cookery. I. Title.
PS3569.E8 Z87 2000
813'.54—dc21                                          99-055970
[B]                                                          CIP

First Picador USA Paperback Edition: January 2001

10  9  8  7  6  5  4  3  2  1

*I long*
*to be with you where angels dream*
*of ginghams in the lily-spangled dawn.*

# Contents

# 1

## *Cynthia*

MY MOTHER ONCE SAID that all recipes were launched with a sautéed onion. She tried everything to mitigate the stinging tears. She canvassed habitués to the house for tips.

- A piece of bread held in the mouth—not to be eaten, Cynthia, but clamped between nun's lips;

- The onion held under cannoning water while being peeled, with extreme caution, because the water obscures your vision, and it's difficult to do this with nine fingers or eight;

- Only the top end of the onion lopped off, leaving the root end intact as you chop, because the chemical warfare originates there at the roots.

Short of tying a kitchen towel over her eyes, my mother found the only real solution was to pour herself a glass of red wine and chop the onion as quickly as possible, throw it into the pan, blot her tears, and stop grumbling.

Every night.

She was a good cook. People remember that about her. Oh yes, yes, she wrote several novels, received acclaim, battled cancer, raised five children. But she was a good cook. She was a good cook not because the feeding of a family of seven, plus routine entertaining, and the importation of odd sojourners into our house for months at a time beat the basics into her. She thought about it. She cared. The edges of her intellect weren't blunted by the tedium. When the umpteenth layer cake for a child's birthday party slopped over to the side, she was distraught. Forget the publishing date. Forget the school play. No number of flagged toothpicks would persuade the top half to sit happily on its layer of jam; it skidded. She made another cake.

"That's what you did," she would say, referring to the era in which she was the girlchild, not the mother, and girls were channeled, like small tributaries, into a common riverbed. "That's what you did." You bought the proper mattresses, the right tablecloths. You served coffee in the family silver. You dressed for going outside. You behaved yourself.

*Behaving yourself* meant cooking without grumbling, and doing it well. We heard about other kitchens where mothers employed arsenals of boxes and cans to placate empty bellies. My mother arched her eyebrows when we described sugary troves of soft pink things in friends' pantries, or meat in cans. She couldn't duplicate it. Wouldn't. In my mother's kitchen, meals were constructed;

2

they didn't unfold from a seam. It was a mark of pride that cas-seroles and cakes were produced from scratch. And as the butter softened to room temperature, she might dash upstairs to change the linens (where the mark of pride was cotton sheets, no fitted corners). As the soup simmered, she might sit in the library dis-bursing checks. As the dishes dried, as the roast sweated, she would settle at her desk to write books and letters. She seemed to live in her kitchen, making forays into other parts of the house and world. She was there first thing in the morning, a piece of the landscape in her fluffy quilted bathrobe, making coffee, set-ting out ten slices of square bread, top-bottom, top-bottom, to make five sandwiches, plus ten cookies into five napkins, plus five nickels for milk money, for five lunch boxes. She loved a slice of coffee cake, hot out of the oven, and she usually had breakfast ready for eight or more takers, because people stopped by in the mornings, and regularly a woman came to clean, and the occa-sional handyman was always offered warm fare.

That's what you did.

That's not what her daughters made of their kitchens neces-sarily, but we were raised in the recto-verso era of no channels, no riverbeds, no guiding topography whatsoever, only an open terrain in which to run circles or straight lines, or to flop down as desired. My mother worried about our freedom, about us wan-dering across that infinite steppe—finding paths where there were no markers, making moral choices where there were no rules. The human spirit required complications, she said, places to go and not go, ascent and descent, stone walls and smooth paths to or-ganize itself. She explained all this while peeling carrots.

And if we were not there dangling our legs under the kitchen

3

table, she would have told someone else. If she were alone, she would practice new French phrases. She'd consider names for characters in her novels. She would stop shucking corn cobs to find a pen and jot down a line, and then she'd go back to the corn, or at least that's where her hands would be occupied. You never knew where her head was. The Mediterranean. A mini-skirted daughter painting red fists on the yellow brick walls of the high school. The end product was fresh sweet corn, fresh chopped liver, fresh spaghetti sauce.

"Spaghetti sauce comes in jars now," I want to tell her. I want to see her face.

"But it's so easy to make!"

"Nobody makes it anymore but your daughters."

I chop the onion until I can't see from tears. I throw it into a pan to crackle alongside a few bay leaves. *Bay leaves. What is the French for bay leaves?*

When I miss my mother, I miss her in her kitchen. It is the room I return to again and again, to pull at the cupboards and open the refrigerator door in my mind. Which was the old tin flour drawer? I'm wondering, because the mounting years have interfered with what was once familiar, thrown modern and heaping details of life's progression in the way. I see myself tripping over them, tripping over the new memories as I have tripped over roots that rise up from trod paths. Down! I command them. Roots are for under. Memories are for under. Yet these newest details rise up above the soil and are sturdy in the open air, like the first fish that walked onto the shore to breathe there, too. They clutter my trail to the earlier days.

It was to bypass the scuff and tumble of almost fifteen years of intervening data that I wanted to go back to the house on Harrison Avenue and find my mother, my memories of her. I wanted to run up the back steps and sit at my place at the kitchen table bench, and let my eyes drift across this panorama like the visitor to Sissinghurst who longs to sit alone in the tower room, as though *place* were a time machine and could carry one back to an afternoon of voices quarreling in the entryway, or to the noise of a pen scratching without pause across paper. I wanted to hear my mother sally across the kitchen floor humming Ella Fitzgerald songs while lugging a roast to the oven. I wanted to see her figure at the stove again, whisking flour into a gravy, or at the sink, with her back to me, the bow of her apron reminding me how she had made life practical and pretty at once.

It was a big kitchen, in a big house, which seemed only just large enough to encompass the seven personalities of our family, personalities that remind me now of cumulus clouds, big and fluffy, ready to rain, but vapor really, and assailable, vulnerable. One boy and four girls grew up believing it was more useful to speak first—a question of self-defense—and worry about walking later—no hungry hyenas in the hallway; and so we filled the seventeen rooms of the house with years of opinion and argument, writing our lives over and over like biographers given one sheet of paper. Not that our bursting commentaries were ever taken too seriously. No one forgot, in our house, who was the parent and who was the child and who was to be seen and not heard, and sometimes not seen.

There were treats, moments of unrestrained license. My mother used to let us crayon the walls before she papered them.

We wrote our names, drew our alphabets, created cities, fought over square feet, made horses and pastures, sketched out the big yellow house with the boy and the girls, big to little like xylophone keys, and all of their dreams. When our arms were tired and our crayons had been reduced to pebbles, my mother arrived with her brushes, ladder, and rolls of wallpaper. She pasted heavy strips of florals over our excited expressions, entombing them, smoothing out the wet paper with the soft palm of her hand as she would smooth the tears off our young cheeks.

"James Thurber used to draw on his walls," she murmured once, sealing up a room in gold foliage. "Imagine living in a house of illustrations."

No one ripped off my mother's wallpaper, years later, in a heated search for hidden drawings. My father finally sold the old house to two women therapists, reputedly lovers, one pregnant, the other an heiress. They needed no added illustration. They wanted "an important house," they said to my father. The heiress's mother drove up from the city with an architect, leaving her chauffeur to sing to himself in our driveway. She coursed through the rooms with visions of walls falling to create suites, doors exploding from exterior clapboards, a grand kitchen emerging from the horrible thing at the back of the house.

My mother would have been the first to shrug them off. Tomfoolery was better than skullduggery. She, who identified herself as pre-Sputnik, had had fewer choices in determining her life, while nowadays women had too many choices, so many opportunities to make poor choices. My mother would have chuckled about the noisiness of younger generations of women, the way they cast about hunting up a snazzy identity. She called herself a realist, would have painted like Vermeer; but she would never have painted a kitchen.

"Don't romanticize," she cautioned me when I tried to turn high school into high opera.

*Revisit Jumieges instead,* she would say now. *Our kitchen is gone. Take your memories and run.*

I took my memories and two wooden spoons, thin and flat from years of use. My own children chew on them now and they are for me like the silver rattles handed down through generations and dented by first teeth since the time of royal blood.

*Don't romanticize.*

I didn't put the spoons in my safe deposit box.

*Let it go,* she would say.

But I can't. I have let too much go. I have too little left, and now I can't even go back to see the old kitchen. It doesn't exist. The red linoleum tiles were pulled up and there were indistinct rumors of terra-cotta.

"I love terra-cotta," my mother would have said graciously, thinking, but it's cold for infants to crawl on, and everything shatters when it hits.

The little radiator where we dried our mittens was wrenched from the floor to make way for better things—like ambient heat. Of course, it never was up to the task of throwing heat into that cavern of a kitchen; it was only good for drying mittens, leaving puddles of melted snow on the floor to rot the tiles and timbers. It was a radiator with a Napoleon complex, too little to heat the room but ready to burn you if you touched it—not the shade of history anyone wants to re-create in their kitchen. And the coal stove is gone, yanked, in as much as five-hundred-pound iron stoves can be yanked, with grunts of satisfaction from the heiress's mother's architect's knowledgeable house wreckers. My mother would have sighed a bit about that. She had come to love that stove. She and Molly, her best friend around the corner, cooed over it and the way it was Emersonian, no, Dickensian, no, Medici, no, Byzantine, no, Aristotelian, no, hunter/gatherer— yes, hunter/gatherer to have a real fire in the kitchen, a real fire on which to cook. When Molly popped by, my mother would put the old tin coffeepot on the stove lid to reheat a bitter cup for them both. If you were going to make coffee in an old three-piece tin pot, with paper toweling as the filter and unnumbered editions of reheating, then the next crack at putting a fire under it wasn't going to do meaningful damage to the taste. These were hunter/ gatherer days after all, and it was convenient to have a coffee-maker that could withstand the primitive heat element of our coal stove. Molly used to giggle about how well my mother had stoked it, and she promised not to tell anyone, like a husband, that the entire iron lid glowed orange from time to time in the early months of the stove's acquisition, when the shoveling of coal lumps and the proper angling of the damper weren't sciences or even arts. My mother used to chuckle that she was keeping West Virginia solvent and half its male population employed to keep her in coal. Privately, she worried that she was keeping the whole state in an iron lung.

So there would be no kitchen to go back to, no familiar size and shape and smell. And it was fantasy anyway, because my mother died years ago, and when it became my father's kitchen it removed itself from my attachments, became other, even before the other of the two young women. My mother would have applauded my father for his rearrangements, his efficiencies, the way in which he took up soups and began farming out his own tips to all the children. Not many men stay bachelors after losing a wife. My father did. When my mother died he slowly fit his life to continue without her. He moved into the kitchen. Over time, she sifted out of it.

That's why it didn't matter about the two women and their important destructions. That's why it didn't matter that they rearranged the entrails of our old house until it became a grand boudoir, at which point, word has it, they materially divorced, and the heiress decided to leave psychotherapy and get into real estate, and I never asked what happened to the poor child. Boudoirs will do it every time; boudoirs and all those other misdiagnosed dreams that take us through the sluices with passion, and at the end we wake up, exhausted, stripped of select illusions; but still we feel compelled to pursue the trail of passion, as the physicist pursues the trail of energy, if not in this corner then maybe in that one, because energy never dissolves, it only transforms itself. So we may chase passion in our youth, or we may be chased by it, but there comes a day when we don't want it to bother us anymore; and it has been reducing all this time, a soup stock boiled down into something denser. Finally it dries up, loses its oils like an old chestnut, and becomes altered. We have aged. Passion has aged. We both become less transparent and we can sit quietly together on the front porch and laugh about the old boudoirs.

My mother loved bread, round and tawny and warm as a cooling ember. She considered herself a European at heart. She was ready to get back on the boat and undo what three generations before her had done, because the Proppers of Czechoslovakia probably wouldn't have sailed here had they known about the lousy American bread.

There was an old Polish bakery on Pleasant Street, almost out of town, that made fresh rye bread. For years it was my mother's pilgrimage so that she could have cottage cheese on rye toast for lunch, not every day, but almost every day. Then Mrs. Naumann opened her pretzel operation in the back of a brick office complex on King Street. Mrs. Naumann imported her flour, imported her salt, imported her bakers, trained them, and started them on the pretzels, which were heaven, and then expanded over the years until she was right downtown with a variety of fresh European breads and pastries and a legion of bakers, who eventually fled her tyranny and started bakeries of their own. In the midst of this entrepreneurial thunder, Mr. Naumann also fled and started a new marriage of his own.

My mother tracked Mrs. Naumann's baguettes from sidestreet to main street. She made noises to my father about the up-and-down quality and the up-and-up prices. The practice of slipping one of yesterday's tarts in the box with three of today's piqued her sense of morality, but the slapstick image of one guest at a party whacking away at tart #4 was a kind of recompense, as though the great comedy of life made amends for life's less honorable moments. I patronized Mrs. Naumann's bakery at my mother's side, tap-tap-tapping away at the glass case, my finger aimed at dark things, chocolaty things. If I made noises about the diminishing size of the croissants, my mother would hush me. *Noises* were for adults in the privacy of their homes.

"Let me remind you," she would whisper in my ear while our *ble*—a bread shaped like a sheaf of wheat—was slipped into a long white paper bag, "that the Mrs. Naumanns of the world are pushing forward the envelope of possibilities for the Noras of the world."

Mrs. Naumann took on a new stature for me then: The woman who marched onto Main Street, the woman who didn't always behave herself, or who redefined behaving. Mrs. Naumann had turned her kitchen into something industrial, brought Old World recipes to New World machinery and stamped out hot coins in her stainless steel ovens. Not that she was a model of content-ment, if the feminists were keeping score. She couldn't keep a baker. Customers fishing nickels from their wallets would clear their throats to mute the sound of her screaming in German, French, and English, from below, in the big not-so-happy kitchen. *These pretzels are knots! The linzertorte is burned! A raise? Breads rise, not salaries.* And so there was a history of exasperated young bakers ripping off their flour-coated aprons and stomping out the shop's front door, and if you peered down the stairs you could see Mrs. Naumann tying an apron around her waist and assuming command of the dough.

Mrs. Naumann made her kitchens seem like cold, pounding places. Forges instead of hearths. Of course, they made her a lot of money; forges may, hearths won't. The whole town crowded her doors in the morning, grumbling about the fact that for a German one might expect her to unlock the shop at precisely eight o'clock A.M. But she didn't, and this was troublesome for an academic town that thrived on Polish jokes and was kind to its Jewish population, and was ready to honor Germans in the

name of Beethoven and Dürer and forgive Mrs. Naumann her
heritage if only she would sell her marvelous breads with respect
to the little calendar of hours that she had posted on her plate
glass window. Then, just when some of us might have renounced
her kitchen and gone elsewhere, she started providing full meals
to accompany the lovely bread, and seduced public opinion back
to her side with frothy cappuccinos and neat espressos. Perfect
timing, in retrospect, because people were looking for excuses to
cook less, abandoning their kitchens as they abandoned their
families and communities. It began when they cluttered their
countertops with machinery to save them every step but the
choosing of the recipe. Then came take-out and vacuum packing,
and it all toppled over after that. Hooray, then, for the Mrs.
Naumanns of the world who agreed to provide us with the good
food that many of us decided not to provide for ourselves.

But "Oh!" she would say to my mother as she gently fingered
the fine skin of her eyelids. "I was such a beautiful girl. Look what
has happened to me. Divorce has aged me!"

Naumann's Bakery turned into a kind of voting booth: If you
shopped there you were on her side. She would tell you her husband's latest courtroom atrocity while filling your box with strawberry tarts. Then, glancing down, her eye might catch a tart
whose berry had been jammed like an afterthought mercilessly
into the custard. Fury. Off she flew, downstairs to the kitchen to
fire the baker outright, and often you would lose your tarts in the
commotion.

On the order of not losing sight of the forest for the trees, it was
best in Naumann's Bakery not to lose sight of the bread for all the
distracting tarts, éclairs, German curses, and cash register bells. My

mother bought her loaf and savored it, but regarded it as a complicated product because she couldn't separate the bread from the Naumann, as most women can't separate a thing from the multitude of connections and connotations that swirl up in a dust storm around it. It gave one pause for thought—the bread, the bakery, the kitchen—that *professional* kitchen where people were paid to cook with dispatch, not saunter, where yielding heaps of pale dough were slapped and rested in silence, where there were refrigerators and ovens, like yours, but bigger, and not white but gleaming steel, and, well, it needed to be said that the food may have been delicious but it was not made with you in mind. There. The hard truth of buying food already prepared. The baker didn't know you. The saladier didn't know you. Maybe even Mrs. Naumann didn't know you, counting out your change through woeful eyes. You could be eating the result of someone else's deplorable day.

So wasn't it better to head home to your own kitchen, and plumb the refrigerator for just a little onion to sauté, because once it was crackling in the pan and you had poured yourself a glass of wine and splashed half of it into the pan as well, you could make anything taste good. And it would be there just for you, made for you by a caring hand, a fresh warm meal for a solitary soul, something hot for something you don't want to go cold.

⌒

*Once upon a time, Molly lived around the corner forever.*

That was the fairy tale. In one sentence, two women from two worlds became inseparable friends. Molly and Cynthia kept each other's daily diaries, using the quick cup of morning coffee or the leisurely glass of afternoon wine for their ink. They recorded.

They carefully forgot. Light, like a cleaver, split the hours when Molly and my mother leaned toward one another at the kitchen table, and when it was my parents, upright, presiding over a meal. Punishments were milder by daylight, the walls and rules became pliant, the air resonated with the snapping of dry laundry and the rippling scents of baking. By late afternoon, forts melted into couches, firemen wearily trudged into the bathtub, Indians sent only dreamy smoke signals and all bears snored. Molly went home to cook for her husband and daughter and we children yawned into books while we waited for our father. Molly's presence in our kitchen was a part of daylight, and her absence after six, when our father came home, was a part of the night.

When my mother's response to the bakery wars downtown was to stand by Mrs. Naumann, buy a fresh loaf each day and make bread pudding once a week with the stale bits, Molly, the progressive, started making her own French bread in a spanking new food processor. God knows how virtuous that was. My mother would have been the first to say, Wasn't she lucky to have this virtuous best friend around the corner who made fresh French bread? Because my mother had a few lines drawn in her kitchen, and one of them was: No yeast shall cross this threshold. Indeed, it was perfectly silly for her to bake bread, all those hours, when there was so much else to do that no one else was doing. Like writing her books. Like teaching her children to behave and wishing there were some way to teach the rest of society to behave, too. Improving herself, her children, and the rest of the world, kept my mother quite busy, kneaders of the world be damned.

Molly taught music at the local community college. She had one child, Emma, to my mother's five, and she was younger and taller and full of pizzazz and did those wonderful trendy things like own a food processor and use it. She had thick jet-black hair down to her shoulders, and when streaks of gray began shooting through it, she experimented with colors. She, like my mother, marched into the bathroom with a box of rinse, closed the door, and fought it out with the gray and the mirror. By lunchtime they might be sitting at the kitchen table with less gray, or in Molly's case, with a head of curiously orange hair, or one time, green.

My mother would silence us with a finger drawn across the throat if we mentioned Molly's hair. Fair enough, but if anyone were to have green hair, or orange, it should have been Molly, who could carry it off with her black sunglasses, tall lilty figure, and Mississippi drawl. She made green hair a kind of dare—a rhetorical *doesn't that just taste like sweet cream?*—that made you think twice, hmmm, green, when normally you wouldn't think once about where green did and did not belong on this earth.

Molly's kitchen table was square, a plank of glass over pretty caning, and usually covered with breakfast litter late into the afternoon. I'm sure my mother had rolled over in bed at least once, and said to my father, "You know, she doesn't clear the table from morning to night," so that she could hear the sound of it and decide whether it was a conspicuous accusation or a hairless remark. After all, Molly was younger and came from somewhere else, and my mother was ready to suppose it was the rules in our house that might have to change, until she could resolve to her own satisfaction that it was the codes in other houses which were questionable.

Molly got a coal stove for her kitchen, too, so that she and my mother would have warm backs wherever they chose—her house or ours—to eat Brie and bemoan low thermostat settings. She was in and out of our kitchen door almost every day, and on the other days my mother would be settled in Molly's kitchen, her back to Molly's coal stove, picking up the threads of conversation the way women pick up their needles and continue to poke and purl and knot through their lives.

"How are you, Cynthia?" Molly would smile as she swirled hot water in her red kettle.

And my mother, never one for sweeping open-ended questions, would clip: "Fine, and how did Emma do in her swim meet?" or "Did you finish correcting exams?" or "What do you intend to cook for Saturday's dinner party?" and so forth. Then my mother might recount a trip to her publisher in New York City, lunch at the Algonquin, a small room at the Carlyle (blue pumps and a Donald Davies dress), a grand adventure for a serious woman in a world of patriarchal and enamored men, while Molly giggled and murmured "no!" and "did you!" in between sips of hot coffee.

My mother did most of the talking. She orchestrated the dialogues. She sent probes into space and waited and listened across the light-years of kitchen time while the radio signals bounced off Molly in Alpha Centauri. Alone afterward at home, my mother would wash salad greens and consider what she'd heard.

"Friendships take work," she would say to me.

I watched my mother send out her probes with many visitors, watched her launch and receive remarks, but I never thought Molly took work. She was so easygoing. She was like a lanky figure on the runway modeling serenity, a broad smile, a swish-swish of her skirts as she slipped into place at our table, never anxious, fielding my mother's signals as though she had expected them, lovingly, while tracing pine knots in our kitchen table with a tranquil finger. I thought Molly was easier than the rest of my family, who recorded and recounted life with a jeweler's eye and a jilted lover's passion. Molly's version of life seemed more relenting than ours. She seemed to pull, *whoa*, gently on the reins. She sugared life, the way my mother sugared our bitter grapefruit halves at breakfast.

"They're eating oat bran over there," my mother once notified my father about Molly's household. She was testing the waters. We all knew Molly's family "kept up." "She buys organic milk."

Then, "Why do you suppose she doesn't offer us a loaf of her French bread from time to time?" My mother might murmur this at the sink with the faucet going full blast on a heap of spinach leaves and her back to us as though it didn't matter, because her friendship with Molly really had nothing to do with the rest of us. It spanned no more than the two souls who defined it and only dusted their husbands and children.

Even so, there were moments in their history that frayed them, that tested the seams of friendship and forced them to recognize weak stretches in the fabric. One time Molly's family took on a puppy that was mean, which became a dog that was mean, and my mother felt it wasn't right to keep a pet that bit postmen and children. My mother argued and pleaded to have the dog put to sleep, but Molly wouldn't hear of it, and my mother was left to bite her lip.

"What is reasonable to one ear is inconceivable to another," she would say. She had tried to win the battle but her opposition was dug in; and my mother knew there were times when you had to stop fighting, when it didn't matter anymore who was right and who was wrong, when it was time to salvage what the salvoes missed. She pulled out her troops. By the time the dog bit Molly, on her face, my mother was unable to utter a word.

After my mother died, I was the one walking along thin sidewalks rippled by frost heaves, crossing the corners of grassy lawns, and wending my melancholy way to Molly's back door and into the kitchen. If the dog was loose in the yard, slavering for a taste of somebody, I'd call from the street until Molly came and collared him and locked him in the basement. I climbed her back porch steps looking downward, as though I might find the silhouette of my mother's practical shoes and plant my feet in her footprints, making their way through winter snows and spring mud, and follow her inside.

I never came to Molly's house knowing what to say, unlike my mother, her mind a perpetual broth of topics.

"You have to keep people interested," my mother would tell me. "Ask them what they're reading."

*Groan.*

"Then tell them what *you're* reading."

But Molly never made me perform feats of friendship, like being interesting. She would amble over to her kettle, put a fire under it, and brew up these powerful cups of tea that smelled of wood burning, and we would talk for an hour or two about my mother and the vast hole she left behind.

"Tell me about my mother," I would say to Molly. And she would sigh, or make some noise that satisfied and deflected, until I began to do the chatting, the storytelling, giving Molly my memories the way my mother had given her recitals.

"You are so much like your mother," Molly once said as I headed down her steps into a dark winter's evening. The notion swirled round me like pink and black ribbons, snapping pleasure and menace at my bones. I ran down the streets toward home.

"*You* became my interesting topic, Mom," I blew into the raw air, my insides clenched to hear some signal, a sigh, an ironic snort.

I leapt up the steps to our empty house desperate to inhale those last lingering motes of her presence before the next vacuuming or the next wintry gust swept them away, replaced them with scentless dusts.

Years passed. The young grew up and the grown-ups aged. Molly continued to teach music and buy organic milk, and her daughter eventually graduated from college, and I was far from home when Emma called my father one evening to say that she had been sexually abused by her father from the age of eight to fifteen, had been threatened with death if she told, and had her head dunked in the toilet to prove it. I suppose she called him to anchor her story in my mother's lagoon, that body of warm safe water into which we all tacked now and then, as though to find her, lashing our ropes to our father instead.

My father sat and listened and said to me later that he was only relieved my mother hadn't been alive to hear it, the details, the log book, the iterations of what did and maybe did not happen. Trauma is a violent editor of memories and publishes in the most destabilizing way a biography of nightmare and personal history, so that the memories become one, like the many trunks of the banyan tree, and no one can ever say that this trunk is truly the tree and the others are superfluous or secondary; finally the only thing left to do is surrender the whole tree to some new purpose, a marketplace maybe, so that the women of the village may sell their wares on its fat roots and history may remember the tree differently, kindly.

Our family was reminded that whatever you know of a person within the trunk and tendrils of a friendship, it is only two percent of what there is to know, and that you live together on the surface of the ground, only vaguely aware of the vast structures underneath. We reached out to Emma as we felt our mother would have done. Molly no longer came to our kitchen, and I went no more to hers, because whatever I believed of the facts and fictions that continued to drift dolefully through our house, and whatever icicles formed in my mind from the wintry drip-drip of Molly's innocence or acquiescence, it was Emma who needed a kitchen table to belong to now; it was Emma who needed shelter.

There are pieces of your life that you are sure will never sink into the quicksand of history, and there are people with whom you swear you'll never lose touch, and there are plans you make, benchmarks you set, promises sealed by spit on the palms. And then they are forgotten. Bit by bit they topple backward soundlessly, get swallowed up by a swelling past, and all those promises to yourself become as meaningless as the dust that settles on your bureau. So, Molly tumbled backward soundlessly into my history, as did my oaths to remain in contact with her, as though history were a great hungry maw.

Without my mother to hold us together, in presence and then in absence, the magnetic bond between Molly and me gave way. It was only a larger movie version of the little story in which molecules swirl endlessly around each other, losing atoms and gaining others at the expense of those surrounding, in a play of self-preservation over time.

Emma became unreachable, as perhaps she had to, putting distance between her past, which contained a bit of my own, and her future, which needed to be built from all new materials. She couldn't trust me enough, because I materialized in her world as her mother's friend.

"You can't have lunch with me here, and then go have lunch with my mother," Emma once said to me, sealing me off with another brick and a little more mortar. I didn't debate it with her. I didn't want any more earth to tremble under Emma's feet.

And now, I cannot make a cup of that charred woody tea without thinking of Molly, without wondering about her innocence, her loyalties, her belief in what happened and didn't happen. I wonder what color her hair is now, and who is the recipient of that wide-armed Mississippi grin.

"Lapsang suchong," I want to drawl to her, like a password that would fling open a door to happier days, and she would know that I had found a name for that smoky tea she used to brew, and she would giggle, "Well, there it is," in the open-gated way she had of embracing people, always providing them with an exit, and always with a way back in. She would never restrain someone, and maybe that was part of the problem, because Emma had staggered out the back door one day and Molly had let her. My mother would not have asked for the truth, only solution, that Molly find some bridge made of string and beads or steel and stone, but do something, anything and everything to rescue her, to get Emma back, because she was her daughter.

I keep this box of Lapsang suchong in my cupboard, face forward and right up front on the shelf although I rarely use it and curse it occasionally when I have to reach behind it and things topple. It's a rough and tumble kind of tea that you don't drink alone, but only in the company of special friends who will love it for its strange strength. You may as well steep the ashes and wood shards in your fireplace as drink this tea, except that wouldn't bring me back to Molly's kitchen, with my back to her coal stove, watching her slowly whirl the water in the red kettle while she listened to my narrations, murmuring phrases of love and support without beginnings or ends.

I didn't know how much my mother loved Molly until I became a mother and came to love my women friends with the almost unconditional love I had for my children. When I turn up in their kitchens, with child in tow or without, melancholy or chirpy, I am reminded of Molly at my childhood back door, peeking in with a wide, expectant smile to find my mother's form there. I thought I would see her broad warm face for the whole of my life, that I would one day burst through her kitchen door with my own children for her to love. She would give them a hunk of her freshly baked bread, and compliment the bow on somebody's dress and appreciate somebody else's good manners, and it would be as much a full circle of life's attachments as could exist for me.

But she is just a shadow presence now. I see her smiling, raising her eyebrows, and drawling *uh-huuuh*, as I reach into the cupboard for tea. She is saying yes to all my resolutions, even those in conflict, because she was going to walk down each and every road with me, applaud each and every thought, consider but never decide.

~⁓

A shadow presence is what Frances called her little boy, her fourth child, born without a brain and doomed to live out his two years in an institution. He became a shadow presence in their family, she wrote in a letter to me, years later, after Cynthia died, and after I lost my first daughter.

I always wanted Frances to love me, because she and my mother had loved each other so much and for so many years, but she didn't. I think she didn't even like me much, in the way you can't ever love any children but your own and there are those of your best friend whom you want to love, but can't, don't. I never resented Frances for not loving me, although I never stopped trying to hook her.

Every summer since I was born I would see her. Her family lived in Virginia and met up with ours on the Outer Banks of North Carolina, in Kitty Hawk, in rental houses that sat near each other on the dunes. It took us three days of driving to arrive at the Outer Banks, a vast sandbar with a few small concrete roads that took you from home to pier, to Winks, the one grocery store, to Anderson's Trading Post for a newspaper three weeks old. There was a phone booth at Anderson's and pails for carrying potable water from the road up to your house. Kitty Hawk was just sand and sea oats then, a kind of suspended heaven on the water. The army tested mortars a few miles up from where the concrete slabs of road fell off into the sand. On the bay side, protected from the harsh Atlantic, shrubs grew into dense forests, Spanish moss dripped for dinosaurs, and crabs sidled up from the water to pinch your car tires.

My mother and Frances would both bring down their recipe boxes, although my mother's box inevitably got misplaced or forgotten in the first few days, while Frances's box, stressed, presided on her kitchen counter from the first moment. It was twice the size of my mother's, plain and plastic, which made good sense in a seriously spattering kitchen. Frances followed recipes. She read the numbers and measured with a knife. My mother's gay little box sat on the kitchen counter for two weeks emanating low-radiation ideas. Measuring interrupted my mother's sense of vacation. It interrupted her train of thought. She preferred to send my father out for fresh crabmeat and box brownies.

The two families spent each day in the sand, flowed into one house toward evening for drinks, then funneled back into separate rivers, each family to its own house for the night. Only my mother and Frances were inseparably joined in a kind of endless conversation, finding each other in the mornings after the families had been dressed and fed and sewn into that tideline on the beach where the sea embroiders fresh stones and shells and seaweed each night. The children would play at the water's edge while the two mothers brewed each other hot black coffee in the rental coffeemakers and discovered the magic of putting a dollop of ice cream in the coffee instead of milk and sugar. This entirely wonderful ritual had been conceived one day after lunch, but moved gradually backward in time as though synchronized with the tide clocks on the walls, until it was eleven in the morning when they were pillaging the rental freezers for vanilla ice cream.

24

It was the pattern of their friendship, the repeat in the cloth. They would settle their families and steal away, acting like merry thieves as they tricked life into offering up its pleasures.

Each morning Cynthia and Frances found one another on the shore or up on a balcony overlooking the sea oats, and began talking, while their hands popped the seeds out of watermelon or sliced up cucumbers for salad. They would talk as the day unfolded and the children burned under the sun, and they would talk while they smoothed salves onto our backs and pulled shirts over our shoulders, talk and talk, as though the year in between our summer vacations were a book of empty pages, and there on the ocean they had just two weeks to fill it all in. So I know Frances's voice as well as I know any voice, and I knew it the night she picked up the phone, many rangy years since I had last seen her, when I called to thank her for a gift. Her voice, like a wind catching up the leaves, brought something of my mother back to me, because my mother loved that voice, and my mother's voice changed when she heard it and laughed alongside it. Each summer, two voices on an ocean, singing like a love song for two long weeks.

*Did you talk about the little boy?* I want to ask my mother. *Did you call Frances each year on his birthday?*

Because every baby carves a path across its mother's heart, from the moment she dares to glance up at the bathroom mirror and catch her own eyes there, King Solomon's eyes, telling her she is responsible for another life. Two hearts beat inside her. There is a space traveler crisscrossing the universe within her, composing itself tirelessly from the spare bits of her body, making itself the center of her interior cosmos before it emerges, nine months later, and she becomes its sun. But those babies don't always arrive sound, and the mother's universe implodes and no hole is as black and vast and frightening as a mother slumped in the sod beside her child's grave.

*Was there a grave?* There, in the warm Virginia soil. Did she lean small toys against the cold marble? Did she bring back shells from Kitty Hawk to set in the moundless grass?

But we never knew, we children, because the death of a baby is a melody played softly through its mother's life like an intimate dirge, and you have to have died a little yourself to hear the music.

I thought Frances arrived at Kitty Hawk joyful, free of phantoms, thrilled to have two weeks with my mother, ready to fry crab cakes for twenty. Her grocery bags bulged with unfamiliar treats and the things that sprawled across her countertops were different than what stretched across ours. Bags of okra, homemade mix for hush puppies, Damson plums for jelly, the grand Smithfield ham, jars of pickled watermelon, barbecue sauce, all turned up in her kitchen in North Carolina. She called applesauce *lumps* and threw things into it that broke all New England applesauce rules; and lumps tasted better than its finely sieved cousin, and fresh hush puppies tasted better than anything.

*Oh, Mama, please!* we begged. *Make those for us, too!* Though it was foreign to our kitchen—the cornmeal, the deep frying. My mother would try, but she warned us that things taste best where they belong—red Burgundies in Beaune, hush puppies in Kitty Hawk—and she was right, except for one thing: lemon chess pie. This pie transcended time and place, and my mother liked to make it because it reminded her of summer in Kitty Hawk, with Frances.

And this is the recipe from Frances, as written down by Cynthia:

## *Lemon Chess Pie*

Oven to 350°

| | |
|---|---|
| 2 cups sugar | ¼ cup melted butter |
| 1 tablespoon cornmeal | ¼ cup milk |
| 1 tablespoon flour | 2 lemons touto |
| Salt | 4 eggs |

Beat like mad for a minute and bake in a preheated pie shell.

I have given this lemon chess pie recipe to friends, and most glance up with a querying look. Instruction, they want, which to mix with which first, second, and third. Yellow or white cornmeal? What if the lemons are small and dry?

"Touto?"

"Be reasonable," I say. "Juice and zest."

"Can I buy the juice? Can you use those jars of zest?"

"I have no idea."

"What about the crust?"

"Don't you have a steady crust recipe? Doesn't everybody have a trusty crust recipe by now?"

By now. My age. Thirty-eight. Halfway through life as I see it, although my family has a history of lives curtailed. I would have thought that halfway through your life, a woman's life, you would have a reliable pie crust recipe. If you didn't, then every apple pie and quiche and chicken pot pie would pose unimaginable anxiety for you, because it doesn't seem to matter if you're a doctor or a lawyer or an Indian chief or a Native American chief; if you're a woman, you're expected to be able to produce a palatable pie with little to-do and less notice.

The lemon chess pie is simple and remarkably delicious. When I make it, I make it for my mother, and she is tying my apron strings into a bow and flouring my counter to roll out the dough. She is modifying the recipe as I go along, her eyes catching the dearth of lemon zest and my hands rummaging the fruit bin for another lemon. The cursory directions are hers, her sensibility, her humor, her thick love for Frances. So Frances materializes in my kitchen, too, and the two of them start giggling about something shared as though they were young mothers again, with cropped hair and bright red lipstick, remembering pregnancy and the hot fudge sundaes at Howard Johnson's *after* the doctor weighed them. They met after the Second World War, on the Yale football field, among all the other expanding young families in half-Quonset huts set out soldierly on the rectangular playing grid like Christmas logs on a baker's broad steel counter.

In those Quonset huts, "kitchen" was really a euphemism for the whereabouts of the sink. When you entered the Quonset, the kitchen was on your right. You had to close the door behind you to let down the kitchen table, which hooked up against the wall. A small bookshelf was the pantry and the defining kitchen wall. While their husbands were in medical school, Frances and my mother tended their babies there, on the football field, watching their toddlers empty the bookshelf of tinned soups, making tinned coffee for one another in unglamorous aluminum pots, pouring it into modest cups as they poured their words into the air.

They are with me when I make a chess pie.

And why make a pie without company? they chirp.

*How* make a pie without company? my mother snorts.

"It's crowded in here," I smile, breaking one, two, three, four eggs into my bowl. It's crowded in my kitchen. It's crowded in my head.

I wish my mother and Frances could see my children now, Hugh and Madeleine, the next generation of expectant bellies, dragging their toys over to the kitchen floor to wait for their warm slices of lemon chess pie to emerge from the unlikely class picture of measuring cups, egg cartons, and flour cloud. They are emptying the cupboards, stacking pots, investigating the effects of apple juice on crackers, and apple juice on crackers on their mother's nerves. It's my children eyeing their mother as she sings snippets of old songs poorly, chuckles, shrugs, talks to herself; and it's my children, now, who think their mother is crazy.

I never supposed my mother was crazy, really. The fact that her thoughts were always elsewhere was too much in harmony with the tenor of our household to cause alarm. Not paying attention to the child with you was, in my mother's book, almost a badge of sanity, and talking to herself resembled gratifying dialogue in a house full of children. Still, I thought my mother was crazy not to want to spend more time with me, and worse, I came into the world unprepared to share her in fair proportions. I needed her there with me while I rolled, crawled, wobbled, ran, trampled, and grumbled on the red linoleum tiles of our kitchen floor. I sang to her as I emptied the lower cupboards of staples and pots. I hung annoyingly on the refrigerator door. I rubbed scrambled eggs in my hair, and smiled, so that she would love me all the more. I pointed out years of dirt on the undersides of surfaces that no one else was short enough to see.

"I can't wait until you're taller," my mother would sigh, and then she would get a big hot pot of ammonia water and go at it, the stove hood, the bench at the kitchen table. "You're the only one who plays down there . . ."

I spent my early childhood refusing a virtual meteor shower of bribes to entertain myself. We struck bargains around the house. I could stay in the library if I was quiet. I could bring my toys into the kitchen if I did not protest her singing Judy Garland songs. We would go apple picking if she could stop on the way to buy new yarn.

She was clever in making her contracts, and I was fierce in enforcing them. If we had agreed on Ella Fitzgerald, then no Sinatra—and no singing along. If it was one stop for yarn on the way to the supermarket, then no second stop no matter what.

"Imagine living with such a tyrant," I would say to her now, pulling out the pie dish, finding a child's long-lost cloth animal behind it. "Maybe I should use the larger quiche pan."

"You weren't a tyrant," she would say, the softener of truths. "You were . . ." She would hunt for a word, shrug, smile, say nothing. "Use the quiche pan. The recipe is for a large pie dish, and it slops."

She worried privately about her children, the anger of one, the loneliness of another. But she didn't worry with extravagance.

She wondered why they did not address their pains the way she had: Spot them, prioritize them, dispatch them. She didn't spend much time measuring her woes the way we do today. She bottled her fears and went forward. She didn't wallow in the courtesan guilts of motherhood; she wanted to know why a child didn't take life into its own hands and make it better; she wanted to know why society didn't protect parents from adolescents.

"Mama," I would say, hugging my awkward adolescent self with a mixture of hatred and pity, "I'm so unhappy."

"Who said you had to be happy?" she would reply.

She was tough, that one.

It was what her father, Karl, used to say to her, and the ordinary philosophy of it had assuaged her, had soothed the hurt, maybe, or at least given it a proper cubbyhole when her own mother, Charlotte, called her Little Stupid. Charlotte was tough. My mother was tough. How surprised she must have been to give birth to several children, not all of whom were so tough. She must have mused about it—as she yanked the skin off chickens, pulled the peel off oranges, scrubbed the film off mushroom caps—the range of vulnerabilities, the way bruises penetrate apples so quickly, visibly, while you can play football with a butternut squash and cook it that night. But then she would giggle, the absurdity of a football analogy making its alien way into her head . . .

The lemon chess pie filling is fluid, like pumpkin pie filling. It's nice if you have help opening the oven; inevitably some sloshes.

"Slish slosh," Frances would say; the two of them, with a hundred lemon chess pies between them, recollecting that each time you had the final fluid in the mixing bowl there was always some edge of concern—so thin a soup. It was best to pour it into the preheated pie shell near the oven because ferrying this yellow watery nectar across the room without having it slop over the edges was impossible.

When my mother got ready to put pies in the oven, every child crawling, toddling, or running across the kitchen floor could sense a change in the atmosphere, a low-pressure system rushing into the room, stilling the noise, tensing the mother.

Why does it matter so much? I would like to ask her. After the graduate degrees and the marriage and the childbirths—after all those hoops, why does it matter if the pie slops a bit? Because it does matter.

Having said that lemon chess pie is easy, I should qualify. Some day, some wonderful one will invent a machine, smaller than eight cubic feet including the motor, able to fit in most immense kitchens, not too loud if used in conjunction with a car muffler, that takes the zest from lemons and oranges and not knuckles. But my personal woes about citrus zest pale in comparison with the timing issue.

After about forty minutes, you have to open the oven and jiggle the rack a bit, to see if the center is firm-ish. The top of the pie should be brown and there will be this thin aureole of bright yellow around it, brilliant as a solar eclipse but in brown and gold—gold where the lemony sugar pulled away from the crust. It's a pleasure to watch, to stay at the helm, there in front of the stove, watching over your pie because your crew has gone to sleep and you alone are responsible for seeing it into safe territory. I always feel like this in the kitchen. I can't leave because

I'm never sure when something will be done, underdone, or over-done, without being there. One foot out the door and something might be bubbling over, charring, congealing. I read the instructions in the books and on the boxes. They tell me *al dente* means nine minutes; they assure me I could go for a walk; they say six minutes to wilt, two minutes to sear, and twenty minutes at a simmer. But nothing beats being there. A recipe presents a hypothesis. You have to test it.

Timing a lemon chess pie will never be science.

"So much isn't science," my mother once said to me. She wasn't baking a pie at the time. She was trying to tell me that the cancer was back, that the earlier treatments hadn't been cures, that medicine didn't have a solution, yet.

My mother liked people to stray into her kitchen. She liked to talk. And oh, the innocents with whom she would find conversation! First she would cajole them with her cheeriness. Then she would draw them out on some subject of mutual consideration: the aging of a parent, the next presidential election, the price of heating oil, and, heaven help us, the impatience of children. There they would be, opening their hearts at our kitchen table, perfect strangers, when my mother would take off her disguise and assault them with the applicable commentaries of Plato, Hegel, and Braudel.

"Have you read . . . ?"

And their worried faces would wrinkle into bewilderment as she regaled them with the awfully useful philosophies, which she was just reading herself, and which perhaps could offer some succor. It was her concern that would reach them. Her concern was real. Her caring sailed like an arrow through the mist of her own unintelligible words, and then farther, through the miasma of their own unarticulated pains. Life is full of clouds and arrows, contours and lines. The right word shoots through so much chat. The right spice screams to you from the midst of a dish. If you have never put nutmeg into minestrone you might not understand.

"You're the local Statue of Liberty," I would grumble, as she served hot breakfasts to the humble and weary who stumbled through the kitchen door, many of whom hadn't maybe identified themselves as wretched until they bumped into my mother that morning. They all felt safe undressing in our kitchen, figuratively speaking, and it was only when the mailman actually tried taking off his clothes there that my mother constructed some walls.

Well, she might say now—now that I was old enough to be told, now that the years had made him a poor sod instead of a frightening specter—there probably weren't a lot of people who were nice to Frank.

*What did you do? Invite him in for coffee cake?*

She would reflect. He must have had such a dreary life, dropping letters at closed front doors, day after day. No human contact. And there was my mother, with a warm smile and a hot drink for everyone whose empty life seemed unbearable to her, suddenly finding herself sandwiched between the washing machine and the freezer.

*Did you fight him off? Did you scold him?*

She wrinkled her face when I asked about it. She was trying to remember the steps, the chronology, after years of turning so many lives, including her own, into novels. She recalled that

Frank was a simpleton, just sound enough to walk letters to doors, and that when he found himself one freezing February day in our kitchen, with my mother offering him a hot half-cup of coffee, he began to do what he thought men did when not delivering the mail. My mother shooed him away, gently, without moralizing.

Eventually my mother lost her energy for every next pilgrim. When her babies stopped crawling across the kitchen floor and began walking across it and running out the back door, she annexed some time for herself. She pinned an "Overpopulation" button on her coat, and from nine to twelve each morning she settled in her library to write. It was like a new Age in our house. The Kitchen Age was over and the Worldly Mother Age began. To her young children, it felt like an Ice Age. The traffic of handymen to our kitchen door tapered off. We moaned from the lonely kitchen table. We brought toys down the hall to the library, on tiptoe, but were sent away. Sometimes my mother even closed the library door, as best as it could close, it being one hundred years old and regardless of heat or humidity dug in its heels two inches shy of the door frame. My mother believed that discipline was the larger part of achievement, and she proved it by pounding out book after book in the short intervals between bouts of cancer.

I engineered my own boundaries while trying to modify hers.

"Mama," I would mew from beyond her library door. "Mama, I'm bored."

"Read a book," she would shout out to me. Later, she would say, "Go to a museum. Listen to a Mozart concerto. Visit the botanical gardens."

"Mama, let's do something."

"I'm working now."

Sigh. "But I'm not." I was free. I was ready to be entertained.

I can see her leaning toward Frances, the two of them snapping the ends off green beans with their fingernails, and my mother sighing, "This last child, this fifth, is so needy."

What my mother never suggested was that I cook. She did it so often and so well and so without complaint, that maybe she forgot. Maybe, having fought for feminism through her books and daughters, having fought harder for her life, she thought the kitchen was just too inconsequential to merit serious education. After all, a woman may plant her body there day after day, but her mind should be sprouting elsewhere. Which is how my mother trained the minds of her daughters. We all learned to cook smart and we married men that liked what issued from our kitchens—which was smarter still.

I learned from her how to create those happy little Maginot Lines that keep a home in proper function: Mother here, Father there, and children way over there. I do the cooking for the household, spend my days in the kitchen, and do anything but encourage my own children to help me mix cookie batter or shape a meatloaf. Better those precarious towers and tunnels made of spice jars and Tupperware than a child with a spoon and a bowl of wet batter inside a house. Better jelly in the cabinet hinges than a child's little fingers pushing bread crumbs into meatloaf tartare and tartare into mouth.

Once in a while I break down and invite the neighborhood children to push raisins into gingerbread figures in our kitchen. When I watch these small bodies intent on their business—their art—their tongues frozen outside their mouths in concentration, I'll mention a provocative thing I've read in a book.

"It seems all the galaxies are zooming away from one another," I say.

One child looks up at me and eats the raisin in its hand. Another pauses, having heard amid my noises the particularly fetching word *zoom*. My children, schooled, ignore me.

I have stirred only the air, perhaps as my mother did when she offered me bits of Ortega y Gasset while she washed the salad greens. But it sufficed, for me as for her. There is a loneliness to enlightenment confined, and as my mother blossomed she was bursting with a need for better company, so she tried to make her children better companions.

She tried to get us thinking early, to assure herself that someday we could think around the tedium and sorrows and mailmen that would walk through our own kitchen doors. Good training, in retrospect, for the day that cancer tramped in to stay.

~

It was cinema. The familiar head popping into view, at a diagonal, cocked with inquiry. At just past eight every morning, pushing through a rushing current of children off to school, Don Rogers would thump up the back stairs and tip his curly white-blond head at the kitchen door.

"Anybody home?" he would bellow, merry as Santa Claus and similar in stature, a kitchen door for his chimney hearth and bountiful presents of humor and generosity for all the children. Don filled the doorway, ducked slightly as he crossed the threshold, and stressed the bench at the kitchen table as he levered himself onto it. He never broke the bench, but he broke chairs over the years, so many that my parents began buying larger, sturdier chairs for the house. In the library, on the screened porch, in the kitchen, there were Don's Chairs, and children's bottoms scrambled out of them when he happened by.

I was often in Don's Kitchen "Chair" at eight o'clock in the morning. Five years old, wide awake, ready for a day of my mother entertaining me, I would be perched at the end of the bench. My mother would be trying to interest me in her bird book, trying to catch me up in her passions so that I didn't become an obstacle to them. Our bird feeder hung just outside the door and no number of sparrows deterred her from checking the markings in her little guide.

"Did you see a spot of red under the wing?"

"No."

Or, ten years old, wide awake, picking at my mother's slippers annoyingly while trying to rouse her concern over my dislike of tuna fish, and shivering because of the odd color of her skin weeks after chemotherapy.

"Maybe you'd like it with relish."

"No!"

Or, fifteen years old, wide awake, waiting alone on the bench for Don while my mother was back in the hospital, and flipping hopelessly through her bird book, still trying to catch on. My mother thought that a love of wisdom was just a matter of catching on—the vagaries of birds, asymmetries in Greek architecture, the French school of historians. For years she shoveled information my way, one metaphor after another.

"Do you get it now?"

"No!"

You knew Don was coming because the acorns in the driveway would pop and scatter under his big black shoes, or because the birds fluttered from the feeder, and after them, reluctantly, the squirrels. He thundered up the steps even in those days before the weight became more destructive, before his knees and feet went, before his pancreas finally gave out. He climbed those stairs bearing burnt Christmas cookies from his wife, or the first tomato of the season to show off; he leapt up the steps like a soldier climbing out of the trenches, and later, like a veteran, slowed by his canes and crutches, over the sheeting ice, finding a foothold among the slick autumn leaves. He hopped into our kitchen until he hobbled into it, at just past eight in the mornings.

Don's size defined him—the way he filled doorways, the generosity of his person, his stature in the community, his armament against life's sorrows, the number of hearts he sheltered, like Giotto's Mary, a loving immensity at the altar enveloping hundreds of souls within the folds of her blue cloak. He was everybody's doctor and he was the favorite doctor, the kind who still came to see a sick child in its bed, who made you laugh so hard you would forget to tell him what hurt, except your sides, from laughing. He was the doctor who overlooked bills for those who couldn't pay. He was the doctor busy giving the neighborhood's cats and dogs injections of penicillin that made them loopy for days. Don fixed things. He kept girls' secrets. He became the county medical examiner, doctor at the county jail. He sat on state boards to decide where the monies would go. He planted tomatoes in the summertime and mums in the fall. He made strawberry-rhubarb compote once a year from the rhubarb in his backyard. He managed to find joy in his routines.

Every morning he would wait for my mother to offer him a cup of coffee, and he would sigh, "Well, that would be lovely, Cynthia," or "Just half a cup, maybe," or "What a nice idea." One time he switched to decaffeinated coffee and my mother ran out to buy one jar of it, instant, but not a big jar, knowing how long Don's bursts of dietary self-improvement lasted. There were times he declined a slice of coffee cake—the weight, you know—and sometimes my mother would snort because it was going to be another week of watching his intake and then none, or because turning down the cake at eight o'clock and having a shot of whiskey at five was really hopeless; but often enough she applauded him, because she wanted him to slim down, become healthier, stay alive, in case she didn't.

"tonyjuliemaggiejennieNORA!" my mother would yell from the kitchen. "Dr. Rogers is here."

I would race downstairs and throw myself into his bearish arms. It was the custom in our family that the children's near fatal ailments were recounted to Don at the kitchen table, while he listened with head cocked, sometimes pulling a stethoscope from his jacket pocket, sometimes chuckling from the flowery descriptions.

"How can you not be feeling well, Nory? You're too perfect!" he would bellow cheerfully.

He would be squeezed onto the edge of the bench, waiting for a cup of coffee while I regaled him with the horrors of illness: My spots—"freckles"—aches—"growing pains"—it hurts right theeere—"nothing." Then I would feel much better, and because of the very high fever, which I would have forgotten to mention, I would be delivered a nice plate of buttered toast, edges trimmed, and cut into long strips. That was the treat for ailing children in our house. The extra trouble. The strips. No crusts. Very satisfying. Very curative.

It took the sweep of one forearm for my mother to make room for Don. She would brush aside her things, brush aside the peace of the moment for the love of conversation and friendship. She brought him his coffee and carried over her sewing basket. In the evenings, over wine, it would be her knitting basket, but in the mornings, in light of five children, there were always buttons to replace, hems to let up and take down, labels to affix for summer camp. Sewing made her giggle. Once, somebody's rooster of a father had asked familiarly, "Cynthia, when did you decide to write?"

And she had answered, "When I found out I couldn't sew." A line that sent her ever afterward into peals of laughter.

So my mother sewed with irony. She sewed quietly as Don sipped his coffee and narrated the tales from his world: Prisoners at the local jail were making obscene phone calls from the pay phone; town junkies were following the hospital garbage trucks to the dump to find needles; a body was found in a closet; the emergency room staff was feuding with the postoperative staff, still. Sometimes my mother would look up from threading a needle and make a light noise, having spotted a rip in Don's jacket, and say, "Take off that jacket this minute." Don's split seams and the buttons that popped off his raincoat were a part of our lives. He never interrupted his stories to pull off his jackets.

"They put a Nautilus machine in the jail to work off tension and now I've got four sheriffs escorting convicts with pulled muscles to the emergency room . . ."

"Don, this whole seam is gone. You need to get some suits that fit."

"They get to the hospital. They like it there. They start lobbying for elective surgery, moles removed, ingrown toenails . . ."

"Don!" my mother would snap. "You've got to stop that silliness at the jail. And you've got to lose some weight."

My mother ran a house. There were no bureaucrats in our house, no red tape, no codified rights. It was an amenable tyranny, like Babar's. Don's stories infuriated her, and what saved the spirit of the morning's coffee was his merry laughter at the end, like the lilt of an accent, throwing its timbre upward like two querying hands.

"Ah, well," he would say. He had brought the lunacy of the world into our kitchen, the stories of the wayward into our room of security, to laugh at, both of them, the wayward and the secure. He was doctor to both, had to care for the bruises of both, found compassion for both. This was one world, this was another.

Don's house was one world, our house was another. In one world was his wife and mother of his five children with a thick Viking's braid down her back and a determination to burn shortbread for the neighborhood each Christmas; in the other was a woman in a fluffy bathrobe who loved to catch a cardinal at the feeder and who made leaping, querulous analogies between the hordes of dull-plumaged species that devoured the seed and sociological disappointments in mankind's history. In the one house was a dog that chased squirrels and postmen; at the other, squirrels bulged in the rectangular cavity of the feeder like animals inside medieval letters and by sheer greediness found a place in my mother's allegorical histories because there are always elements that are larger and impossibly routed. Don watched over both women and all ten children. Growing up, I thought Don was really ours.

We thought Don would go on forever. We needed him to fill the doorjambs in our lives: In our kitchen, in his office, in his examining room, his tall figure in a white lab coat, limping, later, after the knee and foot operations, his stethoscope dangling somewhere on his broad chest. He seemed unstoppable, despite the cane, despite the thick corrective shoes, despite his heft. He found a new kind of rhythm coursing down the sidewalks of Harrison Avenue, his still thick and curly blond and white hair bobbing. At seventy-one, he had passed the stage in which loved ones would urge him to lose the weight and slow the drinking.

Then one day, the feeling gone in his left foot, his face mottled with the exertion of walking, he was told the latest news. He hobbled up the front porch that evening for a whiskey in the library with my father, my mother's rocking chair empty now while the two men sat in silence.

"Paul," Don said to my father, "my luck's run out."

He had been diagnosed with pancreatic cancer and given six months, six uncomfortable months, to live. He began the process of tidying up immediately, preparing his family for his absence, winding up those affairs that could be cupped into completion, and finding a home for those that would go on. He closed his office, found doctors for those patients who had never been able to pay, took the framed Brueghel prints off his waiting room walls. My father sent me newspaper clippings from the local paper announcing his retirement. Even Don sent me an invitation to a big party in his name at the hospital; it was in the same envelope with a note of sorrow, because my baby had just died. I longed for one of Don's huge enveloping hugs. I worried about my father, on the brink of losing this forever friend after already losing my mother; and I felt trembly, watching the pillars of my past crumble just when my future had fallen in.

Don outlived his six months by a small margin, and he did it without the full complement of agony diagnosed. I saw him that summer. He was hobbling still, but he'd lost weight and seemed rested, restful. There were no tomatoes in his garden; there hadn't been time to plant that spring, in between operations and recovery. But there had been the unvanquishable rhubarb in his backyard, and he made the compote my father loved one last time.

"They tell you two cups of sugar, Paul," he confided. "But I only use one." He jotted it down on the back of a prescription paper. 4:1 The secret ratio, cups of rhubarb to cups of sugar. Very nice on coffee ice cream.

He had taken up piano lessons just after his own doctors had determined his hapless diagnosis, and his first thin booklet of sheet music was dotted with cheery stickers from his teacher. We sat on his back porch and he pulled the soft sheaf of melodies from his briefcase, pointing out to me the problem sections, chuckling at the occasional sticker with a frown on its face. Then he walked me home, two doors down the block. That was my world, with Dr. Don Rogers two doors down for as long as I could remember. At the end of our driveway I was desperate not to be left. I would never see him again.

He hugged me tight, sopping up my tears with his shirt.

"You'll be all right, Nory," he whispered.

I sat in his chair at our kitchen table and wept.

Life was to be learned in the kitchen, in our house. Learned and absorbed. That's where most scoldings took place, where little ears overheard what they weren't meant to repeat, where little sisters stumbled upon big sisters with b-o-y-s. I first heard the text on sex at the kitchen table, aged twelve, having woken up that morning with little more in my head than images of cinnamon raisin toast. Some drops of blood on my underpants derailed me. I walked somberly downstairs to my mother, who was sitting at the table with some sewing in her lap, and said, "I have to tell you, I'm going to die now."

That became the morning of the Big Discussion. My mother was as taken off her track as I was. She couldn't believe no one had informed me, child no. 5, daughter no. 4. And I hadn't bargained for this shock ever. My mother set aside her sewing. She chuckled nervously, but she was up to the task.

She didn't say, "Welcome to womanhood," or "I'm so proud," but rather, "I can't believe I forgot to tell you." She didn't say F is for Female. She didn't embrace me as though this were some wonderful moment in the longevity of women. It was, after all, the beginning of inhibition, the realization of vulnerability, of responsibilities, of an internally laid slalom.

What my mother did was launch herself into a description of evolutionary biology, Darwin, seeds and eggs, the larger context of male and female species—where women fit in, where I fit in, where men fit in—first figuratively, then, with stammers, literally. The description, the idea, the process, outlined alternately in grave tones and giggles, was worse than preposterous—it was horrible. She made a circle with her thumb and forefinger to show me the diameter of an erect penis, then said, "But a little bigger even," and opened the circle to give me the proper terrifying proportions. Finally, seeing me mute on the edge of the kitchen bench, she took me upstairs to clean me up and show me the procedures, what girls did, what women did.

Oh no, not my girlfriends.

*All females.*

No one I know.

*No one escapes. Escapes is the wrong word. It's a nice thing.*

Wrong.

The kitchen table looked different when my mother led me, shaken, back downstairs. She offered me buttered toast cut into strips. Maybe she didn't slice off the crusts this time, now that I was a woman. One half hour into womanhood, I sat still as stone and looked around the old kitchen, checking for signs of further betrayal.

Ours was a big kitchen by any standard, squarish, in a big old squarish house. The washer and dryer and freezer rubbed elbows and made noises at one another in one corner. They grumbled about being segregated, like second-rate machines, about being penned in by a half-wall, nearly counter, mostly bench back, that stuck out from the real wall like a Corps of Engineers jetty built into the middle of a little square pond. Over this half-wall sat our kitchen table of soft pine, with knife ruts and black knots that ruined a child's penmanship. It was wrapped on two sides by a built-in bench, and on two sides by chairs. The other half of the kitchen was workspace: oven, counter, cupboards, sink, and refrigerator. There were four doors: one to the backyard, one to the basement, one leading into the pantry and then the dining room, and one sending you into the center of the house. The kitchen was the heart of the house, a muscle pumping people into different parts of daily life.

It was not modern. There were simple wood cupboards with flat faces and layers and layers of paint on them. Olive green. Blue. One year my mother visited Giverny, and soon my father was painting the woodwork yellow. When new appliances were ushered into the kitchen, there was familial fanfare, proper murmurs of admiration, some kicking of the baseboards, a torrent of reprobations concerning little fingers staying clear of the disposal, little hands not fiddling with the oven face, little noses not loitering at an open refrigerator door. Of course, the defining moment in our kitchen was the arrival of our first coal-burning stove, Chappe, named for its maker, a small brown enameled box that made a place for itself between kitchen table and stove. Smug little tinderbox. There was life before Chappe, and life afterward.

I hated Chappe. I hated this stove and the subsequent larger models that arrived over the years. Maybe I was too young to see its charm—a sweet little black-lung machine in our kitchen. Maybe I hated its role in our house, its adoption. My parents purchased Chappe in response to the oil crisis of the early 1970s, when the price of heating fuel rocketed, and when my mother, who had traditionally burned enough oil to warm the whole neighborhood, became Conscientious, tipped the thermostats toward sixty, closed doors, wore sweaters, and dug around the bathroom closet in search of hot water bottles. When I whined about the cold, she snapped. This was a new mother.

Chappe came to keep one central room in the house warm—God save the kitchen. I thought my mother had become a hippie, a poor rendition of a hippie, a wannabe hippie; you had to see it in context, the year she planted potatoes in the backyard garden and walked around with her pitchfork as though she were Mashenka wearing a babushka. I was at that fearful age when the comport of parents was so crucial to profiling the self that any shift in their image seemed life-threatening. I was that age from four years old to twenty.

In my irritable little book, if you had a coal stove in the kitchen, you might as well wear sandals and bandannas and old shirts of unopinionated colors. But that was only the beginning of the changes. The kitchen door was suddenly shut. The central artery of the house was plugged, and when you opened it to brave a new room, a rush of cold air flung itself about you as though it, too, were desperate to heat itself by the fire. Then came the stinging arguments, because my mother and father both thought they understood Chappe's stoking needs best. There was also the coal scuttle, which required refilling more frequently than babies need bottles. To fill the scuttle, one had to descend into the cold, dark cellar, to a baleful cave of a room in which only a bare bulb hung, illuminating with mild horror the cobwebbed cases of wine, forgotten winter sleds, filthy old hoses too stiff with rubber's rigor mortis to serve, and crumbling cardboard barrels with rusted tops ajar, suggesting a kind of dreadful traffic between barrel and room that was too awful to contemplate. There was a mountain of pitch black coal down there, giving any intruder the sense that he had descended into a damp netherworld of spiders and Things disguised as sleds, and old things with sinister claims to not being thrown out, and monstrous engines greedy for coal at the hands of child labor. But there were no greedy engines. Only Chappe. And that's not even why I hated Chappe.

I hated Chappe for making the kitchen unlivable. It was the dust—a fine black coal dust on the table, on the bench, on the cutting board, on the floor, on the round rims of cupboard knobs, on the insides of oven handles, on the crosspieces of kitchen chairs and stools. The washcloths at the sink became dark gray, no matter how caustic the detergent, from a constant wiping up of the dust. There was no more sprawling around on the kitchen table, no crawling along the bench, or flinging yourself with melodrama across a kitchen chair. I felt banished.

"This is bad," I said to my mother.

She would click her tongue. There were larger motives in life—as, for instance, global energy shortages—than a little dust.

"I know that it can be annoying to be told," she once said to me, "but each of us is obliged to remember we are not in Cambodia."

I wanted a second chance to explain it to her, years later. My version: That Chappe was like a cancer in the household, metastasizing black dust. Another cancer. I wanted her to understand the tradition, the transition, the metaphor. But my pain just sprouted its rot in different ways for many years, resentful and ugly, in oblique shafts of anger and distress. She didn't understand at the time, so she couldn't forgive me; so I couldn't forgive myself.

You left me too early, the voice from my center cries out, from the center of the vast and cold red-tiled floor, like a child with its hands raised to be lifted to safety. I was only ten years old when you got sick. Then Chappe threw me out of the kitchen. And don't talk to me about Freud!

But she: "The statute of limitations for complaining to a parent about a parent runs only a few years after high school."

I can hear it.

Once, years after she died, I sat in my mother's chair at the old kitchen table—her chair by day, my father's at dinner. I stared at the back of the L-shaped bench that hooked around the table, unrenovated, unadorned, rising up like a fault line, like the violent thrusts upward of the earth's crust trillions of years ago that left vertical horizons in the ground, to shield her from a view of the washer and dryer and freezer. This had been her topography for thirty years, more than half her life span, with few changes: the plateau of the pine table, the gully of the bench, the mesa of the bench back that we called the Divider, with its litter of skillets, frames, and pencil holders fashioned from cracked casserole pots. In the winters, the coal stove warmed her back. In the summers, the kitchen door was left ajar and breezes would carry in the quarrels of squirrels and robins and cats. The walls were cheek by jowl museum prints, Baskin etchings, children's school projects, because life was to be gotten through and it was important to find its beauty.

It is impossible to suggest that a person could spend so much of his or her life in one room without putting an imprint on it. But could you extrapolate from this surround? I wondered. Could you say that this was her geography, that her being was informed by the broad steppe of open kitchen the way cultures that grew up along the Mediterranean were informed by its weather and waters? The Divider, like a little mountain chain, complicated and partitioned her space, gave her a wall of protection, of definition, like the tiny bookcase that was pantry and wall in the half-Quonset hut those thirty years ago. Or perhaps it was that most of the kitchen's architecture was low, waist level, compelling her ambitions to rise above the twenty-nine-odd inches of appliances and appurtenances, and soar in the thermals of her imagination. And my mother was ambitious. She had been gathering momentum, pounding out more and better books in the intervals of remission, writing quickly because time seemed ruthlessly short. I knew about her ambitions, because I was always trying to trip them up, stop them cold, push them out of the way like one diva trying to crowd out the other. I wanted to put myself in her line of vision. Think about me. Put your energies into me. My needs are simple: I need *you*.

Because there were not two rooms for my mother and myself. There were the two of us in that kitchen. I spread dolls and horses across the floor, and she tacked yellow notepads on the cupboard doors. I did my homework on the kitchen table and she listened to the Watergate hearings on the radio. I said monstrous antagonizing things, and she ignored me. She would have described it as a healthy kind of warfare between parent and child, a tug-of-war the parent must win to save all sides. I played my role well, sulking, moping, whining for attention, training my energies in a quest for more of hers.

Until she got sick, the first time, and her troops threatened a unilateral pullout. It cast the identity of my army into a tailspin, just as the end of the Cold War neutered the cold warriors. I saw the abrupt threat of her disappearance like a terrible remonstrance; that I must not beat my developing fists against her imperturbable flanks, because they were not imperturbable, not in the least, and in fact any slight twist of the wrist might kill her. It was instantaneous, the switch, that I must grow up. I had to do without more of her or I might kill her. Such was the child's version. As many versions prosper in a household as its members, and so close to the identity sits the memory that our versions are what we fight for, forever.

"Don't worry about me," I learned to say, coldly, imperviously. "I'm fine." Because a new relativity blanketed the household; if you were not on the verge of death, you were indeed fine.

"Be a soldier," my mother would say to me. "March on."

And that's exactly what she did, bald, weak, thin, marching downstairs and into the kitchen each morning to put together breakfasts, to sew Don's splitting seams, to insist on a kind of normalcy, a kind of scaffolding and facade, because behind that was only fear and chaos. You didn't give in, as a mother, as a wife. You didn't let chaos in through the kitchen door. You marched on. Life was to be lived until the end.

*By the way*, she might add, for accuracy, editing until the end, if there were to be a last supper for common folk like herself, my mother would order noodles. And so it is noodles I make when my memory of her words is too thin for my ears and her photographs are not enough for my eyes. In those moments I find her through my hands. I tie on an old apron as though wrapping her arms around me and I head into the kitchen to give life to life's pleasures. I pour myself a glass of red wine, sauté an onion, and make noodles.

"Noodles!" she would say. "I love noodles."

I flush with pleasure. My nickname as a child was Noodle, and the word seems like an implicit swag between two pillars of her love.

"No. You were called Noodle because *you* loved noodles." The eternal corrector.

My mother wrote down a recipe for me when I went off one summer, feeling like one of those ninth sons, sent from the house with a sack of flour, two apples, and a reason to make some kind of life for myself.

## Noodles for Noodle

Oven to 350°

One 8-ounce package
  broad noodles,
  cooked
1 generous cup
  cottage cheese (real)
1 cup sour cream
1 clove garlic, finely
  minced

¾ cup finely chopped
  chives or onion
2 tablespoons
  Worcestershire
Salt and pepper
Caraway seed

Throw together in a big bowl and bake 45 minutes. Almost better cold tomorrow.

In the kitchen, I am reminded of the simplicity of my needs.

"Other things can remind you of the simplicity of your needs," my mother and I could tell each other now. "Sickness. Cancer. Kitchens do it agreeably. Death does it cruelly."

My mother knew she was dying before the rest of us. Much became precious—the color of the October trees, the taste of strawberry jam, and the fury of bees that whuzzed above the jam jar. From France, where she was traveling with one of my sisters, she sent me a postcard. It was written during a picnic in Des Bories. Plunk on the address was a pink smudge of jam.

"In my next life I do botany," she wrote.

It was so like her to write that, not that she believed in next lives whatsoever. She believed in dust to dust, sand to glass jar, and plant to strawberry jam. There was just so much she wanted to do and know, and life was so short, even when you weren't about to die at fifty-six. But she was only a few weeks away, and she must have sensed the changes, the shift in harmonies, the tremulous violin sawing of white blood cells on the verge of crumbling, the crescendo of clues leading up to an explosive finale that was acute leukemia.

She fell in Paris. She lived a few weeks more, in a hospital bed. It was a strange house the rest of us gathered in at night, her absence making us awkward intruders in rooms we had already left behind, not so long ago, but long enough that the coals each child had buried in his or her room had cooled and gone out. We butted against each other as we butted against memories. Perhaps she was sleeping as we moved like wraiths in her spaces, but more likely she was wondering how we would make out, then, at home and together, and later, when she would be truly gone. Had she taught us enough, or perhaps shielded us too much, pushed too hard. The house was dark and cold, and the kitchen was silent, and her aprons hung on the hook as though hanged.

It seems strange to find yourself in a kitchen when someone is terribly sick, dying, dead. You are there to prepare food for your hungerless self, or for those passing away, or for their family in the aftermath. There are kitchens in hospital cancer wards where husbands prepare meals for beloved stricken wives. Simple meals emerge. The pots are few, the knife tips are broken, there is no spice cupboard, and you worry about where the wooden spoons have been. But it is a kitchen—sink and stove and little refrigerator. You arrive there with your cumbersome paper bags full of celery and onions and salt and chicken. The bright carrots seem out of place. The spit of sizzling onions seems out of place. The wonderful smell of soup seems out of place. But it all belongs. There are kitchens in the saddest places, reminding us of our simplest needs.

Taste was the one of the five senses that clamored for attention when my mother was gone. Things suddenly tasted different to me, as though, when she had died, there were mourning alterations in my taste buds. I kept thinking about food, about the foods she had loved: cold noodles, hot coffee cake, the glass of red wine in the evening, leeks—if only she could have hired someone to clean the silt from between their layers. And then vanilla ice cream, in the hospital room, soothing her sore mouth as she lay dying. A little Dixie cup after all the travel, all the French cooking, all the literature, all the symphonies, all the children—

vanilla ice cream, what she had spooned into her little children, what she and Frances had dropped into their coffee at Kitty Hawk as though it had been black truffles into an omelet. It was a reminder of simple pleasures and the primary urges behind them.

My children remind me now. They glide into the kitchen saying, "Waaaant . . ." They stand at the refrigerator door like favor-seekers at the temple.

My mother would have longed to receive them in her arms, greeting them with all due gravity, because filling a little belly with just the right thing was important. She would have advanced their cause.

"It was easy with Pooh," she might have told them. "He only wanted honey." Then she wouldn't have been able to stop herself, and, doling out warm oatmeal raisin cookies to two waiting hands times two warm bodies, four, which translated into two open ears times two amenable heads, four again, she would have cascaded into a mellifluous extrapolation about the eating habits of the rest of the plant and animal kingdom. Maybe not Darwinian, maybe more along the lines of hungry caterpillars and somebody's new puppy and bottles for babies and so on. You couldn't stop my mother. But then, cancer stopped her.

Now the daughter takes up the invisible threads of the mother who is lost, secretly dropping spoonfuls of vanilla ice cream into her coffee, not because she has to be secretive, but because she is alone and trying to re-create in her kitchen a play for two actors. She says to no one as she sips: "When the next war makes most of the planet a smooth surface, people will be wandering around, bumping into each other, trying to remember the taste of vanilla ice cream, waiting for someone to offer them vanilla ice cream."

If you say, "Don't go" out loud, you will find that it shoots like a stem of lightning to a forsaken pocket of your soul, illuminating in sudden ghost-white silhouette the image of a solitary child. That's the strange and marvelous divide between words read and words spoken. Novelists exist to ferry you to that child and back in silent story. Poets beg that you read the lines aloud. Authors of cookbooks think that words are only the iconography for a glorious meal. And so, it could be that if you spend enough time cooking in the kitchen, you stand a better chance of keeping that lonely child in a comfortable darkness.

"Don't go," I never said to my mother.

"Let me go," is what she never had to say to me, except in dreams.

Sometimes I know I am going to the kitchen to look for her, and sometimes I feel she is pulling me there to find her. Sometimes her presence comes alive in her recipes. Sometimes her absence casts hoary colors on my walls. Sometimes I am reminded of her sashaying across the kitchen floor with a freshly cooked twenty-pound turkey. Sometimes her own lonely moments in the kitchen echo out to me. There are the memories that I visit regularly, and there are those smaller ones, the unembellished and solitary gravestones set apart from the bunching family plots. They cry out not to be forgotten.

There is something of the cemetery in the kitchen, as though a box of woody tea or a quiche pan would make a better gravestone than a slab of granite or the marble sway of an anonymous angel. In the drawers, behind the cupboard doors, lie relics of a private burying ground that I visit again and again to replenish my memories of love. When I hum Louis Armstrong melodies to

57

the crackle of onions, I am singing a requiem. And when I make my lemon chess pies, I am tossing freesia into the same small river that took my mother's ashes.

History sinks into a kitchen the way fish odors sink into your hands and curries penetrate the wooden spatulas, becoming layers of what is, modifying what was. It settles into a kitchen and launches its spores into generations of other kitchens. Some of those spores are melancholy fellows, but they find cheap lodging with me. I am a great protector of sad memories, a virtual champion of their cause, because even the blithe singsong side of me knows it is the sorrowful moments that shape me. It is finally sorrow that connects us all. So I carry a share of melancholy history from my mother's kitchen, and hold it with me like a rabbit's paw, rubbing it from time to time that its silkiness will trigger memories close to my pith. I carry that history from place to place, along with three old aprons and two thin wooden spoons. When my mother died, pain was all I had left. I have opened the wound myself sometimes, over many years now. I have tied one of her floury aprons around my waist because I wanted the proximity again, because my sorrow is the gateway to her, and opens onto a private garden and leads me up the back steps, to her house, to her kitchen.

Not always were there children on the floor, children doing homework on the kitchen table. Not always was there water bursting from the faucet to fill a big round pot. Not always was the meat grinder schlucking up boiled eggs and chicken livers for fresh chopped liver. Not always were the four lopsided stove-top coils a fiery orange with business. Infants become sixteen-year-olds, usually, and disappear along unpredictable paths into private woods that have grown up around them.

I don't forget my mother clanking alone among the big pots, her last child already in college and now using the front door, not the kitchen door, to come back on weekends to say hello and see if her mother had lost more hair, had lost more weight, had begun to cough again. When I came home, I found her in the kitchen, her back to me, staring out the window, a colander and a salad bowl hanging limp at her sides. She turned and apologized; her head was in a book, she said, but she didn't say which. I knew enough not to believe her. I knew her eyes were picking up signals from deep inside her body, sensing another tumor, or perhaps just the inclination of a malignant cell to take hold somewhere, in her chest, or arm, or ovaries. Her eyes were looking forward and backward, into the future and into the past, watching time in its roundness like crystal balls, as though no point on their surfaces were without vision. She looked and listened in many directions, the way the earth's telescopes and antennae are trained outward into the universe, to describe the galaxies as they are, and as they will be; while the fact is, we see only the past in stars, only the illuminations of things as they once were, and we hear only the noise of millions of years ago through crude instruments of our present. We call it truth, with demureness, as we call our memories true.

My mother was looking into the backyard, toward where she had shoveled out skating rinks each winter for her children, pushing back the snow to make a square and hosing it down in steady succession until the ice was right. She was remembering our gay squeals, five small voices she could pick out in a Vatican throng, our giggles on the frosty air like warm breaths that burst out and disappear, white and then gone, in all the Januaries of time, whenever our patch of earth was shorted of sun. She was hearing those beloved voices again as she stood in her kitchen listening to the murmur of her own death, crying above a bowl of fresh egg salad, because chemotherapy and radiation treatments had rendered her tastebuds senseless and she had poured nearly a pint of salt into the eggs looking for flavor. And hadn't they—the doctors, nurses, the faceless technicians, like pharmaceutical chefs—poured pints of drugs into her, toxic drugs looking for cells to kill, cells precious to her, even though they were renegade. That's the horror of cancer: your own body betrays you, your own cells go awry, your own tissue kills its brethren, making a civil war of your organs in which the cancerous brothers seem destined to win; and you are the mother of every cell, bad and good.

My mother threw out the egg salad, because it was unredeemable. She couldn't fix some things, couldn't add enough, couldn't subtract enough, couldn't correct every soup or salad, or misfortune.

When she lay dying, those last three weeks, there was no talk of taste, no talk of pleasures. She was dying so quickly then, the crisp white cotton hospital sheets falling away from her skeleton like tenting, the toppling of her body by an internal army almost visible to us as we gathered around her bed, the furious energies of cancer using her up; she, the fuel to it, without any hunger during those final days and knowing, like a military strategist, that both sides had only this one fuel in their reserves—her—

and when they spent it, she would be dead, but then at least the war would be over, and the war would not spread.

In desperate moments, I cling to the notion that she is Out There, somewhere, she who would snort if I mentioned next lives. At other times I accept what she accepted, that we are formed from the dust of stars, and to the dust of stars we return. But there is a great magnetism in our expanding universe that affects the alignment of star dust. And we need it. We need order. We need direction.

Mama, you were my North.

# 2

## *Alone in the Kitchen*

A KITCHEN SINK. *Three cloves of garlic. A pan.*

I stand at the sink with my hands in warm sudsy water. Three white cloves of garlic warm in yellow oil on the stove behind me. News of the stock market swirls into bubbles as my sponge circles the bottom of a pot. I muse with abandon. I imagine a neutrino shower bombarding me, subatomic gunfire, zinging against the stainless steel in my hands and rocketing through the kitchen without a trace. I imagine the smell of garlic waltzing through the house, superstring to superstring, reviewing our family photographs and forming an opinion on how I furnished the rooms. I see science, since it spends as much time as weathermen defining the perimeters of its diagnoses, as available to such as me. There are some who wish that science was better protected from the reach of my imagination, but fortunately, they can't reach me.

In my kitchen, I secede from the larger world. I wipe the sound of words like *partisan* and *coupon* from my mind, as I wipe spilled sugar crystals from the counter. I leave my steely intellectual aspirations in the living room and throw salt over my left shoulder for good luck. I blink away the iterations of man's greed and hostility, and my consciousness of my own hostilities and my shames. My kitchen becomes a refuge, out of practicality and out of desire, a cave uncrushed by the daily avalanche of information and concerns, so that I may listen to the news and not despair, so that I may hear of guerrilla warfare and whip egg whites, allowing myself a childlike balance sheet, on which I might offset bad things with good, no matter how bad the bad or how humble the good.

My kitchen is a fortress that would suit an ancillary pope; and there I may direct my attention only to the tapping out of baking soda and the slicing of olives. I can recede with impunity, arguing to myself about the importance of the home, my little papacy, the microsphere, in which what I can influence—and there is so little—is the physical nourishment of friends and family, which is much. You can't reach me in my kitchen, unless I let you. The Great Wall of China is a picket fence compared to my kitchen perimeter.

But these sound like the threats of the endangered, like a raccoon, cornered, hissing its ferocity in the face of things always so much larger—dogs, park rangers, terrified mothers. I have to hiss, to ensure some distance, because sometimes the kitchen is a place of thorough vulnerability, the place in which I sob, drop to my knees, come to understand shock, revile betrayers on behalf of friends, worry to sickness about the futures of loved ones, miss to faintness those people I have lost. You can find me in the kitchen skinned, peeled, sliced, and ground, sipping a glass of red wine slowly, dripping my tears into a soup, scorching a roast, and bumping into counters.

*A clean pot. One red onion.*

I rip the crisp parchment leaves from around a red onion. Is it possible I am going to slice one more onion in my life? I imagine my mother sobbing at the very *sight* of a full onion sack, because it would represent forty-odd years plus one more day of surmounting the tedium and tears. I choose a red onion for variation. If I only had leeks . . . But it has a lovely cupola shape, as though it might transport me to Red Square before sacking my vision with stinging tears.

*One knife. One dish towel. One bowl.*

Red onions are wine red on the outside, translucent circles of white and lilac on the inside. Mine looks like a Christmas ornament, so perfectly round, but it is heavy enough to sag a tree. I slice it down the middle. Flat sides down, it is easy to make thin cuts for my salad. I work quickly, before the tears.

A damp dish towel swabs my face. I smell in its cotton weave the odors of lemons, bacon, soap. Onion bits patter into a bowl. There is no other sound.

I come in from the obstreperous streets and find refuge in my kitchen, the way others find refuge in their gardens. I rinse a pot left in the sink. My hands wrap greedily around an onion as though touch were something mislaid in a world of blinking, revving, shouting, and cash drawers. I pluck a paring knife from the cutlery drawer and let silence, like a feather duster, brush the day from me. I am alone in my kitchen and there is no other nest within my horizon where tiny open beaks tip up to the sky waiting for me to bring food. The notion of small, expectant, wide-open mouths makes me recoil, as though they were not sweet entreaties of nature but the frenzied screams of Guernica.

I must be alone. I must recover from the stimulation of the day—the interactions, the newspaper headlines, the appointed hours, the awkward free minutes. Alone with this red onion, I take in the quiet like a bather absorbing the sun. There is no metaphor for me in this onion, but there is company.

*One tomato. Olive oil. A pan.*

The tomato is mealy. I press it with my thumb and feel its too soft, too granular flesh. My hopes for a side salad are extinguished. I grew up with a horror of disappointing people and have a curious compassion for this disappointing tomato. *Don't worry. Cooked, no one shall know.*

Warm garlicky oil sits in a pan on the stove. I extract the garlic cloves, throw in the onion pieces, and coat them well. They should fry, not steam, so I set the heat high. I'll add the tomato, chopped, when the onions are brown and sweet. I fill my fresh-washed pot with water to boil. I use this pot so often that I wonder at myself when I stow it in the cupboard. It is my waltz partner as I glide from sink to stove top and back again, day after day.

The refrigerator beats like a tom-tom, and the steam from my big steel pot is a smoke signal, and they convey the repetitions of life. It is an art to compel the kitchen to sustain your interest, either by engaging yourself with the process of cooking—the pummeling of a dough or the praying for a soufflé—or by forcing your mind to proceed to a higher plateau as your hands wander through a salad. Tedium results when you posit your head where only your hands need to be. If you can't engage yourself in the dissolution of potatoes into soup, let your thoughts tackle other concepts—a runaway republic, or the figurative approach of Mars. When my mother stirred her onions, she would tell me about the problems of King George III in 1789 and how the rise of the printing press in Europe in the 1600s pushed democratic reforms that much closer. I might have been six. I might have been eight. She knew I wouldn't remember the relevant dates; she hoped I would just remember her doing it, blasting away at the tedium with her thoughts.

She didn't talk to me about the cancer, as though that, too, was a monotony to escape. Perhaps in our household of words, the futility of conversation about her sickness would have worsened the horror, as though what little could be said was no more useful than an ice pick against an iceberg; and no one, especially not a writer, wants to experience the weakness of words, the moment when the pen is bootless against the malignant cell.

*One apron. Two wooden spoons.*

I tie my mother's apron around me and I threaten no one with my scientific or historical theories. That's how I wish it had been: my mother, myself, and the swaying chatter that amounts only to affection. The thought of it suffuses me with pleasure, although I don't look cheerful, there at the cutting board, onion tears still streaming down my cheeks.

The kitchen is about the re-creation of childhood the way you wanted it to be, keeping all that was wonderful in your own early years while weeding out those things that caused pain. We remember the hubbub of women, the warm sweets and hovering smells, the junction of food and love, the wrapping hug of the wainscoting of counters and ovens around the walls, the inkling that one might always find a mother there. The kitchen slips noiselessly into the dreams of our children before they are conscious of it, before they have children of their own, and wake up. Mothers and daughters share the kitchen with a common knowledge of women passing their lives there—at the sink, the stove, scanning the shelves of the pantry. The walls are our backsplash. Our laughter glazes the countertops. Here and there are the scratches that mark our moments of anguish. We cry at the sink, blotting our tears with the damp dish towel.

It's important not to confuse kitchens with food. Kitchens are about process, about the making of the meal, those hours, a quiet retreat or a din of beloved voices, the preparation of a favorite or sacred recipe, like the staging of a private play. I value my mother's recipes not really to taste a taste once more, but to do again what she did once, for me. I stand at the countertop in a floury apron, measuring out, chopping up, sautéing, adding, waiting, serving. When I am alone, no recipe is a means to an end; it is a choreography of connection. The street that once linked my stomach to my heart is deserted and weed-choked. I am cooking to remember through my hands.

My diced Russian cupola is crackling behind me and I work at salvaging this sot of a tomato for the pan.

*Salt and pepper. A glass of wine.*

I shovel caramelizing onions to the side of the pan and throw in the tomato bits and a splash of wine, salt, and pepper. I poke in the pasta pot with a long fork, like a pelican stabbing into the sea with its knifing bill, and I spear a ziti.

I told my mother I would never marry, never have children.

She smiled as though she'd heard it one, two, three, four times before. She said that was all respectable, and yet she gave me a healthy fear of too much solitude. It is the nudge and bump of family and friends, she said, that keeps your surfaces soundly abraded, unpolished, so that you don't harden into something impenetrable, so that your ears will not seal shut, so that your character will not become too crystallized. If you don't marry, she told me, you have to work harder at making sure the Social Interaction is there, because you don't wake up with one.

The pasta is ready, the sauce is ready, but my appetite is poor. I like to cook alone, but I don't like to cook only for myself. It was the process that fed me.

With my elbows on the counter, I stare out the window at an unprepossessing view. Time unrolls like a red carpet before me, suggesting that it is magical to preserve one's life unmarried, childless, with measurable productivity, uninterrupted nights, solitary kitchens and broad steppes for the mind to wander. But I carry my mother's warning like a flag into the country of my solitude. I look for guidance in her books. I read her handwritten recipes over and over, and walk through them myself, the way I used to dress up in her clothes, slip my feet into unimaginably high heels, and scuffle through the house tossing her scarf over my shoulder and saying, "Yes, yes. Quite, quite. Thank you veddy much."

# 3

## *Senta*

SENTA WAS SWISS. She lived in four rooms on the first floor of a villa in Zurich, and for a few years my husband and I lived above her, renting the rooms that she had occupied decades earlier with her sisters and parents—and once there was a violinist, and once two distant cousins whose parents had died of polio, and several times students from the university or wanderers seeking sanctuary. Those were days in which front doors were left open, beds multiplied as if by the magic of sheets, and life's vagaries and brutalities were accommodated, not locked out of the house. Orphans and pilgrims were taken in, another chair was found for the kitchen table, the aged were tended in their beds in the dining room, fruit from the garden was carefully harvested and preserved. Happiness was not something you talked about in those days, only something you might reflect upon in your last years as your history unfurled and snapped behind you like an immense flag.

Senta, who was born at the turn of this century, would tell you that the hardest times were also the happiest because everyone tried their best and no one quarreled. When American bombs dropped not far from the house during the Second World War, the whole neighborhood had crowded into the villa's cellar for safety; and Senta's mother had been ready, fed them boiled potatoes and preserved pears for a week. That was a happy time, Senta said, because all the neighbors forgot each other's transgressions—that Stefan Rubal's cat chased the songbirds, that the Frei twins gathered hazelnuts from Senta's tree, that the whole Britta family parked poorly. Much in the past looked cheery to Senta, just as Rodin's *Burghers of Calais*, from a distance, looks vaguely like dancers.

"Everything is in the world—the worst and the best—and we will have each," she would say, now no longer the daughter but the village elder, her voice wobbly but her huge round eyes still and anchoring.

Among the best were Senta's pears from the cellar, and she would pull memories from those jars with a marvelous suction, as though last autumn had taken refuge in the canning and escaped months later, preserved, into the room; and crowding in like innumerable cousins were other redolent years of her mother's simmering pears and sugar, each time a jar was broken into, the past burglarized when the stubborn rubber ring gave way. Among the worst was the tinned beef tongue that Senta served on December 21—her "special meal," she called it, to celebrate Christ's birthday, if you calculated correctly, which she had by doing some doubtful arithmetic in the margins of her Bible. December 25 was a great error.

But for Senta, the worst was what she saw on the evening news, a killing field to smother the soul. Her hearing poor, she would sit two feet from the screen and set the volume to maximum and watch and listen and leave disturbed. There was that world, and there was hers, and for thirty minutes each evening the one flowed into the other like a poisonous transfusion.

"Great things are amiss," she would tell me. "The planet is in imbalance. And yet I live in peace."

I was looking for peace on my own little planet when I first met Senta, although the daily downpour of her terse philosophical truths was not how I envisioned finding it. I was thirty. I had waited all my life, it seemed, to turn thirty, to put to bed a painful adolescence and a tumultuous set of twenties. I imagined serenity would finally drift down over my small history like thick low clouds over a battlefield, concealing the carnage and suggesting a more humane daybreak. Hope suffused me, and exposed me, so I was ripe for Senta like the blackberries that grew wild in her garden, ripe for her words to tunnel into my consciousness.

Senta would have told you that life's truth and life's magic were twin sisters ten thousand years old. She believed they existed in a kind of fugue, or web, deferring, commanding, spawning, intersecting, diverging—tatting themselves into a tangled lace that stretched across the tips of alps and lay along the broad flats of shoreline. The air was full of forces that demanded consultation, appeasement, reproach, and shrugs, for Senta's gods and fairies were cast in a human mold. They erred, were moody, had the potential but not the mandate to be wise. And there was

71

Senta, cheery in the middle of this maelstrom, giving over her kitchen to a United Nations of the Supernatural. Her kitchen was a safe house for all energies, a Boy Scout jamboree for influential invisibilities. It had been cleared of paranormal mines in 1972 by an old hunched woman with a pendulum, who found an unfavorable magnetic line running through Senta's bedroom, compelling Senta to move the furniture since there was nothing one could do to shift those cosmic etchings across the earth.

She did homage to her gods as she cooked and pared. She checked the entrails of her cabbages for clues, read signs of luck in the medieval shapes of parsnips, gave thanks for unblemished fruit, and chanted as she watched the soul-saving potatoes boil. She was a princess at the temple, there to read you the oracles of organic food and Christian morality and magnetic forces and Hindu reincarnation, as though she were stirring a pot into which each of the planet's cultures had poured its few simple truths, its powerful unknowns. This was Senta's soup. She dined on the amalgam. She was the amaranth, never-fading.

The first time Senta led me into her kitchen, a haze of fruit flies hung like a mad swirling spume over her countertop, where vegetables from the market and flowers from her garden sprawled. She had been regaling me in the entryway with a Serbian horror, something she had seen on the news the previous night, when suddenly she threw up her thin arms in exasperation and insisted that I take a fresh anemone from her garden.

The door from the foyer had opened with a loud crack, as though untried for years. The kitchen was unlit, an aquarium of steely gray and blue in which we swam alert and silent as pike. In dimness, she searched the heap of cut flowers and lumpy vegetables for a suitable white anemone, rustling the foliage with her old thin fingers the way a breeze might. A marble quiet filled the room, cool and firm, so that the sudden splash of water from the sink faucet sounded like the plash of an alpine spring, and the clink of Senta's knife against the enamel was like a noise from an ancient smithy.

"Peace begins with forgiveness," Senta shrieked to me gaily— shrieking to hear herself, to know that I heard her. I had the sense she was explaining something to me about myself, not about the Serbs.

She said in low tones, "You must forgive yourself, first, before you can forgive others. But how can the Serbs forgive themselves?"

I batted my eyelashes, then batted away fruit flies.

"Look at the Germans," she continued gravely. "They cannot forgive themselves to this day." She sliced off the end of an anemone stem and put it in a bud vase. "Though the Germans make very good knives." Somewhere in the heap of carrot tops and leeks and roses she found a sprig of asparagus fern and edged it behind the anemone. It was simple and beautiful, an arrangement you would never modify.

"The French," Senta said, "forgave themselves immediately. It is unconscionable. I find their cooking too rich."

She made me smile, her mind working like that busy cloud of fruit flies whirling drunken above the flowers. She filled the vase with fresh cold water and handed it to me, wet and spilling, as though the water was part of the gift, as though droplets on the petals and droplets on the glass added to the poetry of it, a remembrance of life forces—water.

Senta rinsed her hands in the sink and smiled at me. " 'Who do men say that I am?' " she quoted, using a tone I came to recognize when she was reciting, not opining, with the statuesque posture of a schoolchild reciting at the podium, hands crossed, spine vertical, eyes cast unblinking above the audience. "I was reading in Mark this morning," she explained, linking Serbia, French cooking, and the Bible like a charm bracelet of her current reflections. She was a good angler, switching flies, determined to catch her fish. She pursued, "Then He asks His apostles, 'But who do you say that I am?' "

And who am I, I wondered daily, and wished there were an uncomplicated answer.

Senta did not ask herself who she was, nor explore what she had found in the refractions of other people's eyes. She did not wonder inwardly but instead took her lessons first from her parents and later from the old family Bible that had fallen into her hands at last, like a weary soldier that had marched on, leaving fallen comrades behind. Senta had been the youngest of three daughters and she had inherited those properties that the new generations deemed too heavy, among them the old leather Bible that had bumped down the gravestone stairs to her table. She laid old eyes upon it through her magnifying glass, and it rescued her from her questions with its answers.

"I am making soup for lunch," Senta screamed pleasantly to me as I stood immobilized with my flower, water streaming down my arm and onto a kitchen floor so old that it seemed cobbled under my feet. "Will you join me?"

It always began the same way: the soaking of the grains, at dawn. In the beginning it was only a handful of hard grains spilled into a glass dish of clear water, resting there at the bottom of the bowl or bobbing on the surface of the water, brown kernels nestling soundlessly in the warm womb of bowl within sink within kitchen. For hours they seemed lifeless, hard nuggets resisting the insistent probe of the water, but by ten o'clock you would see that some had burst, and most would give under the tender pressure of thumb and forefinger. There was a kind of excitement in the sink, unknown as yet to the rest of the kitchen. Life was developing in the silence of this little pool, as the first life on earth once pulsed without notice, without future in fact, the mere existence of a biological force that would need thousands of years to pulse twice, thousands more to replicate, a nucleus, a cell, another.

Senta's soup began each morning with the same wonderful promise of life coaxed from the hard pebbles of barley as they bobbed in the morning sunlight.

"I am making soup for lunch. Will you join me?"

I imagined her spilling two handfuls into the glass bowl, the bowl's rim chipped from years of soups and the harder-than-thou enamel of the sink, that old white sow-belly sink, the first in the villa, purchased with great fanfare for Senta's mother eighty-five years ago. All morning long the grains softened, gave in, soaked up, plumped, burst, spit their gluten and flavor into the dish.

Water is like that, whether in little dish or mountain thaw, irresistible, aggressive. No need to be ashamed of giving way to water, of dying in water, because water is as strong as any god and knows entry to the toughest carapaces. Water would tell you that turtles have four Achilles' heels and beetles are easier to crush underfoot than drown, because water knows the vulnerable points of all life.

But Senta's soup was not a murderous thing; it was life-giving. Mid-morning, when the grains softened, she dropped dried chickpeas and rice into the bowl, which was cloudy now from the explosions of barley and looked more like the Milky Way than a pocket of intergalactic space dotted by a few lonely stars. In went the beans, the rice, the dried chickpeas as promising as plastic marbles. Senta would drift like a dandelion seed into the kitchen, drop in her legumes without ceremony, then leave. Alone, she didn't sing. She didn't sigh. She didn't exclaim. She didn't rupture the silences that resided in her garden and her villa. I knew Senta was home when I would peek into her kitchen and see the silent activity of a soup growing in the sink, as the roses grew soundlessly in her garden.

At ninety, Senta was a sliver of life, a spare skeleton, a flower in the hush of her garden, a kernel of grain bobbing brightly through the day. She had a listing walk, her legs brittle bones carved by years into canes, her gait tipping from one cane to the other. And she needn't have been silent, for she was largely deaf and wouldn't have bothered herself with her own bits of noises.

We lived above Senta in her villa for too short a time. We shared the foyer, where she brought in the seasons as a greeting to visitors: chrysanthemums and coneflowers in autumn, or tangling branches of flame-colored leaves; a fat-burning candle in wintertime, and fleeting yellow ribbons of witch hazel like torn strips of sunlight for the three January days they bloomed; in spring there were dark, lugubrious branches of rhododendrons; and roses, roses, roses all summer long with little pieces of paper at the foot of the vase giving us the names in spidery script—Queen Elizabeth, Dog Rose, Othello. Her garden proffered its mysteries each morning like a deep, green Irish lough.

Magic ensconced that villa, halfway up, halfway down the Zurichberg, and Senta moved through this magical field like a hand-maiden to the forces. She cut flowers for bud vases, flowers for low broad bowls, flowers for the grand vases in the foyer—but only those flowers quite done in the garden, those that were turning the color of wrens' wings and were ready to wither and sought from her a last tranquil shade, a calm interior, a place to sleep. Senta answered to the needs of the flowers and the needs of the birds, for whom she collected cookie sheets full of hazelnuts each autumn, dried them in heaps in the kitchen, chewed them and spit them out into a small dish, all year long, for the sparrows mostly, as they were so bold. She was caretaker of her garden, "my wilderness," she called it, which she served with her shears and brittle knees, pruning and protecting but never interfering with nature's laws.

"I mustn't cut it, for it persists in growing there," she would whisper to me as we stood over an interloping plant.

I could see her among the flowers from my bedroom window, her spring of white hair roped like broom straw with ordinary string. I could watch her in the mornings as she set out grapefruit rinds to lure slugs from the lettuce.

"It is murder, really," she would say to me later, flushed with the exertion and sin of it. "But they would devour my garden otherwise! God tells me under which leaves to look, and so I find them, hundreds of them. I snip them right in half, and it is murder! But somehow it is sanctified."

I would be at her sink, stirring a finger in the small glass dish of water and bloated grains while I filled the kettle for tea, and thinking: If it were really true that Senta's God didn't love His own slugs, then which other of His creatures did He find sacrificial?

Senta's god was flexible, if brutal. He had to share the world with all sorts of magnetic powers, galactic scents, and savage races, like mankind. Perhaps that's why Senta's villa had large wrought-iron grills on the first-story windows, because He numbered only one in the throng of forces on earth and every creature had to protect itself for it was not promised protection. So there above the kitchen sink, old and deep, rose a large window with dripping glass, and behind it an iron grill, with leaves and spikes, casting the shadows of a Roman army across the kitchen floor.

It was not a big kitchen, but the ceilings were so high that it was airy, and the tall window above the sink was generous in conducting light through the iron spears and shivering ivy shiveringly into the room. Sunlight sparkled in the little bowl in the sink, where the grains for Senta's soup floated, brown and white. Sunlight splashed in waves across her counters, where pears and flowers lay like fishing boats in a flat sea. Someone long ago had laid a vinyl cover across the counters and when I dawdled with Senta in the kitchen I pushed at its curling edges and imagined gluing the lot some midnight while she slept, or rather read and wrote, the large windows of her bedroom reflecting her under a lamp in the deep evening.

But she might catch me scratching and pasting—the noise of a mouse. For Senta had selective hearing, and although she could hear the clink of bottles in her cellar when I went to fetch water, she couldn't hear the conversations of her friends, whom she would invite to lunch, "and perhaps that's just as well," she would chuckle to me later, "for they are such complainers."

Perhaps they complained of the aches in their aging bodies, these coveys of eighty- and ninety-year-old women who would hobble to Senta's front door with canes and corrective shoes and proper dresses for a luncheon, bundled into their black woolen coats with silver pins and stepping righteously down this familiar lane between the smoke trees and the hazelnuts like strolling crows. They came with gifts and flowers and arthritis, and sad reports of friends dying. They came for Senta's soup and often brought some nice deep chocolate torte for dessert, having learned over scores of years how deprived a body can feel after a healthful lunch.

I heard them from upstairs because they shouted to one another as though broadcasting their words like seed, hoping a comment or *bon mot* would sail through another's deafness and take root; and none would wear a hearing aid, that last assault on the boldness and beauty of a woman's architecture, decade after decade, from the graying of the facade to the weakening of the scaffolding; until the women reached eighty and would not— would absolutely not—wear that ugly hearing aid. And what was left for them to hear anyway, Senta would laugh, that they had not heard one million times over the course of their lives.

On days when Senta had company to lunch, she, too, would put on a silk dress and sparkling jewelry. She took an old stiff apron from the hook behind the kitchen door and tied it around her skeleton as she would tie a piece of string around her white hair, as she would sometimes tie on old pants with kitchen twine, or wrap cotton rope around her waist in winter to hold in place an enormous sheepskin vest that must have once belonged to her father, or uncle, or large cousin. She had a washing machine in the basement, but none of the linen towels or aprons that hung on hooks behind the kitchen door had made the pilgrimage in years.

Little that had been born in that kitchen had ever left—the old sink, the rickety little table, the floor-to-ceiling cupboards of the rear wall. Time's veneers had layered over them gradually, until they all became one color, a mixture of gray and green and cream, dulling like glass on the ocean floor. One day in the middle of this century, the ice safe was removed and a small refrigerator set in its place. Not long afterward, the wood stove was carried away, replaced with an electric oven and cooktop. The towels, hanging from their hooks like long woeful Byzantine faces, watched silently from the door. The sink, a large immovable Pietà, said nothing. Even the tiniest drawers, like harpies perched at the highest rim of the walls, looked down and were mute. Senta's old kitchen was a museum of antiquities suffering the addition of a Cubist collage. That was long before she bought a toaster oven. Even among kitchen fixtures, what was left to say about new generations and obsolescence of the old, for the old sinks were not always wise and the graying towels did not always have wisdom to impart, but sometimes had only breaths to take and space to occupy; therefore it was prudent to admit the new, smile even at the chrome, or the new might tire of them.

By the time I met Senta, the whole kitchen was in various stages of retirement, like a nursing home with its separation of floors for different degrees of incapacity. The two kitchen doors—one to the entryway, one to the dining room—were kept closed, so that all of the old apothecary drawers and canisters were destined to exchange not only the dusts of their own dried skins but the very atoms of their existence, year after year, until they were but a pool of matter that one day might collapse, and reconfigure into some new form entirely. And within this familiar pool moved Senta, at ninety, stiff as an ancient lark.

Senta had taught English in a girl's school for forty years. She had seen many things. She had lived in Florence and traveled to London on a scholarship. She had taught herself to skate, taught her students James Joyce, and baked and sung and sewn, and those were the memories that accompanied her as she steeped tea and cut the eyes from potatoes.

"When I was young I would take an apple and my skates to school and spend my afternoons twirling on the ice," she said once, slicing apples for a tart.

"After university I studied at the British Library, at long shared tables. If there was somebody whom I did not care to meet, I would order many many books and construct the wall of Hadrian between us!"

She had taken care of her parents first, then her two sisters, widows, until Hannah died at last, finally leaving her alone. Now she was like death's notary public, certifying the passing away of family and friends as she attended funerals, signed documents, inherited, gave away. She was testimony to the shrug of the living, proof that one goes on because you are still breathing. White-haired and frail as the little ornament of straw and balsam wood on her piano, perhaps she had always been destined to blossom in old age, when her body caught up with its spirit, as though it had entered an age which most defined her.

She showed me a photo of her family, a black-and-white gone tawny with the years. There she was in the backyard, which was not always a thicket of flowers, behind her seated father, hands clasped, thin, with a long aquiline nose, black hair, and large round black eyes, looking out at the camera with anxiety and compliance, a young woman, terribly shy, too accomplished, with locked-away passions and private flutterings of the heart. Perhaps that was when they found her, those twin forces of the earth. They found her behind her father, and they suggested to her that life in one strongbox was as good as life in another. And because gods are notoriously selfish, and pluck for themselves what they find to be best on earth, perhaps that's when they spun around her a cocoon of safekeeping. She became their trusted vessel, vestal. The touch of a man and the cries of a baby would never govern her.

One day when I had been helping Senta in the rose bed, she remembered a church social long ago. There was music . . . and dancing after the refreshments . . . and a man, such a nice man, had asked her to dance . . . and she knew, from his dancing, what a very fine man he was . . . and there the lapping waves of Senta's story stopped as they had started, a tremor of the earth come and gone, and she returned to pruning past-bloom roses. I unconsciously looked upward, wondering about the wealth of memories that hovered among the pear tree blossoms like angels.

"I am home now," she would say, not with a sigh but with a vigorous declaration, waving a frail arm about her kitchen. "It is my duty to keep the spirit of my mother alive here." She found peace in the room that had been her home as a child, where her mother had made fruit tarts in the wood oven, plucked geese over a pail, sliced the first pears from the new pear trees that were now too tall to reach without a ladder. Senta made coming into one's own as an octogenarian—nearly deaf, missing teeth, hobbled and bruised, more white than gray—look attractive. She made it seem worth waiting for, this moment of vanity's drapery stripped away, when you begin to glow behind all that gauze. She was able to re-create her mother's spirit, find religion in the bounty of the earth, and turn it into sustenance.

*Tell me what you know*, I wanted to ask her, willing from her wisp of bone and skin the wisdom of those cells that burned with the ardor and promise of coals in winter. If only the balance of her spirit could have spread like a contagion and overwhelmed the imbalances of my world. If only I could have arrived at forty with the transcending peace of ninety, but I couldn't. I couldn't leap over the milestones of time's measured road, couldn't coax the old mosses under her pear trees to grow on my stone pots.

*The garden is my bed and the kitchen is my waking hour. So little matters about the journey, once you're at the end.*

That's what I imagined Senta whispering to me in her silvery voice, in a dream, in a sleeping hour, although Senta would have never said it aloud, so resonant would be the word *bed*, the implications of it to one who had given herself to no earthly man. Why did those gods of hers insist on a nun, I wondered, as though marriage and children would have crippled her resolve to serve. But it was clear that Senta saw herself keeping a small candle lit against the world's winds. She would go to her grave with the knowledge of chastity. She would know what most of us did not, and whatever forces had hounded her throughout her near century of living, had drummed at her to turn her bed of deep sleep into a bed of passion—they had lost. For Senta remained like the young girl who claps her hand on the mother-sewn quilt and smiles, "This is my bed," to a friend. She had never modified the paradigm of her comfy bed to include other tales; she had never distracted herself from the pleasures of sleep to accommodate that realm of the pedestal, the pyre. Children, jeopardies of the bed, alter a woman, force her to look differently at her bed, and show her new little beds of worker-bee sleep and innocence—innocence, like a ribbon sewn in and out of the crib spindles, that she suddenly understands now, owning none of it herself, only able to perceive its splendid prism through her children, who own it knowing nothing of it.

But children never intervened for Senta, and so it was her bed that remained innocent—lumpy, soft, shifted east-west to elude the magnetic line found by the pendulum. On her bedside table was a book about roses, a book about cooking with herbs, and the poems of Keats.

"Simplicity!" Senta would exclaim to me, without prelude, without coda. She would look at me with eyes so round, becoming opalescent at their horizons, yellowing, purpling. Her eyes seemed to leap from her face, as though the larger the exposed area, the more she might see of the past and present and future.

*One pink aster. One pair of pants. Boiled potatoes. Mineral water. Bread.*

"The world has gone mad!" she would say, pulling away from the front page of her newspaper. "And yet I manage to live in peace."

Well, there was the long feud with the pedicurist, but she soon found another. And Herr Hans once gave her a poor haircut, but he was very apologetic. In 1988 the city began to tax Senta for her rainwater by calculating rainfall per square foot of her land. But mostly there was peace.

*Two canes. A pad of paper and a pencil. Four clips to hold a tablecloth on a table. An undershirt in winter.*

When I was alone upstairs, she would sometimes invite me for a dinner of boiled new potatoes and boiled eggs.

"Delicious," I would say.

"Indeed." Senta would set out salt and pepper, but such a look you received if you reached for either, for one needed neither and it was likely a sign of some great internal disturbance if you yearned for spice.

*A cutting board. A sharp knife. A magnifying glass. A rake.*

While we ate together, Senta would regale me with stories of the neighborhood.

"One time Stefan Rubal was very sick. Hetti, his wife, told me. She was very worried. She asked me to look in on him. I brought him some freshly steamed broccoli and this poor man, so accustomed to fine restaurants and heavy meals, said that my broccoli was the best thing he had ever tasted in his life. And he immediately told Hetti to make him more!"

*Two dresses. One winter coat. A desk. A milk pitcher. A pale yellow bowl in which Senta once made a divine beet salad.*

"Ah yes," she smiled. "But beets are almost too sweet. They are gaudy."

*One rosebud in a vase. The apple tree's first apple in a dish, with its worm. One pair of scissors. One large pot. A biscuit tin.*

One day I found her in the kitchen with a huge embrace of flowers from her wilderness. She was making bouquets for her friends in nursing homes. The flowers were tumbled across her countertop as though refuse in a heap, unlikely orts flung helter-skelter, stems and petals splayed in abnormal postures, like lifeless bodies in the aftermath of a battle. Weighted down by old half-peeled potatoes, a clump of carrot tops, and a rusty colander, it looked as though she had interrupted a soup to collect them. Tiny flies hovered and landed across the greenery.

"I have harvested too many," she said to me. Her voice was low and she was rattled. She was Athena reviewing a war she had instigated, sorting through the remains for those she let die mistakenly.

*A key. A washcloth. A lamp.*

"You need simplicity to be happy," she said. "And look at me! I have too many flowers. We have too much. We live with too much. We need so little to live."

## Gaudy Beet Salad

| | |
|---|---|
| 2 large beets, raw and skinned | ½ cup fresh cream |
| | Salt and pepper |
| Half of one lemon | |

Grate the beets into a bowl. Squeeze lemon juice on top and pour the cream over all. Wear an apron, for beets stain horribly.

You must let it sit a few hours before you eat it, although it is difficult to wait.

～

We need so little to live. But we need lungs.

I was living above Senta when my baby died. She died in her ninth month, inside me, with a great set of spasms that sent me tumbling backward, out of life, out of time, out of hope. I hobbled home and sank down at the kitchen table, beside a large window with a mountain aspen outside. The mountain aspen was leafless in the February cold and looked horribly stupid, like an imbecile reciting. Mountain aspens at your threshold are supposed to bring good luck, Senta told me, and it had failed. I stared at it compassionately, like one also put into the wrong job. I cradled my belly, wishing against my own clarity that she were sleeping, feeling so small in that silent kitchen, the only person on earth who knew that a baby girl had just died, and it was my baby, nine months old, but too fragile to make the passage.

In a couple of hours I was blotting my tears with hospital tissues. We all saw the ultrasound. We all hoped against reasonable hope that the baby would move when the doctor nudged her. But she lay curled in a paisley, inert. No heart was beating. No denial breathed. She was dead.

She was dead, and I was her sarcophagus. I was the coffin of my finest love, a live grave. Sickness frothed in my stomach but something was keeping it down, and it was shock. Shock is real. Shock is palpable. Shock suspends the normal simmering of life the way a sheaf of dry noodles stops the pot boiling.

I had the strongest craving to be a child again, at home, tucked between two cold cotton sheets. I wanted to start all over, and not lose my mother, and not lose my daughter. I could smell the dry air of my childhood room. I could feel the scratch of the stiff sheets. I could taste buttered toast strips for specials. I wanted to back up and try again.

"Go home," said the doctor. "Have a glass of wine. Take a walk. Come back tonight."

At the kitchen table, my husband and I sat mute, fearful of the world outside. Eternity was waiting to give birth.

It is a cruel fact that the body can nurture an egg for eight and nine months and deliver you a dead baby. It is a stunning blow to find, at the moment you give birth to life, that it is death that rushes out with the afterbirth. I thought I must surely be caught in an ancient myth, in which two powerful gods contended, and when the one gave life, the other ensured its death. I had a deep sense of immortality murdered. I had a more disturbing sense that I was the murderer.

That evening there was the infusion, and in the middle of the night there was the labor. No fetal monitoring, no birthing room. The lights were low and the fuss was minimal. We made an intimate group: husband, wife, doctor, midwife, and finally, quickly, suddenly, our daughter.

In the gush of fluids and blood and afterbirth, there was only silence. We were given our swaddled little girl to hold for a private moment. We hugged her body, beautifully formed and gentle and breathing no breath. I watched the millennial tear fall slowly down the cheek of my husband. This was our family, and it was a melancholy one. This was our trinity, and it was still and softly poignant. This was the circumference of our world, in the small black hours of the night.

"I'm so sorry," I whispered to her peaceful face.

I had been this baby's earth for almost nine months. I had been her bed, her playground, her kitchen table. When she died, she died in her home. I looked down at her imperturbable face with wonder. Here was loss, like a single bud, condensed, impenetrable, full of the promise of its own life, loss's life, a sad life. Loss was born in the death of a baby, and it was loss that would live on, blossom, perfume our home and lives.

Senta was there when I returned from the hospital with my paper bag of nightclothes and toothbrush, my belly suddenly emptied and my spirit drained with it. I had imagined running into her thin arms with my sorrow, her holding me tight and warding off the ill forces that had had their pleasure with me. I imagined her understanding that the loss of a child was the worst. A bottomless, breathless loss.

But Senta said, "There will be others," too quickly, so that I raged against her unknowing and flung myself into solitude.

She had misjudged the strength of my hopes and daydreams, the way a woman is such a heightened version of herself in pregnancy, vulnerable, full of fantasies and primary and secondary plans. Perhaps Senta had never imagined her own role in my visions for the future: that she would have taken form in this baby's life as a grandmother might, left vivid imprints on the child's memories, spoiled our little girl with fresh berries and dewy flowers and recipes for life's navigation.

How often I had imagined a little girl on a stool in Senta's kitchen, wrapped in one of the tattered aprons from neck to toe, oblivious to the layers of dust and rotted pear peelings and sprouting onions and potatoes, helping Senta to sieve chokeberries for some new elixir. There would have been whole mornings spent in Senta's garden. She would have taught our child where to cut roses, and when. *When* was so important to Senta, whether it referred to the waxing and waning moons, or the few still hours before a storm, or the moment between five-thirty and six in the morning when she said the summer day was its coolest. And after a morning of snipping slugs, Senta might have offered a cup of tea on her porch where a little girl child could sit like a lady in spite of the briers on her socks and the pollen in her hair and the dirty scratches up and down her shins. There, Senta would have explained how the English take tea, so elegantly, about her time spent in London, and the wonders of a Liberty dress—long ago, not anymore, no lovely details anymore.

I had imagined Senta teaching our child the art of putting up pears and making preserves. In Senta's kitchen, much was learned without reading. You accompanied Senta as an apprentice. You watched and listened. You used what you could and discarded the rest, just as she weeded through sacks of old vegetables and cut out spots and found fractions of freshness. You ignored the occasional tinned peas and carrots that she opened, shyly, as a respite to her old fingers. The pudding, now made from a packet, arrived with murmured explanations.

There was much for a little girl to learn in Senta's kitchen: That bread was heavenly with butter and honey; that toasting bread masked its age; that tea was taken plain; that one raspberry eaten alone was perfection. Senta sat down each day to a place mat with a linen napkin and silver flatware. She ladled her soup into a porcelain bowl and poured her mineral water into a crystal glass. It was once her family's fine tableware, but she saw no point in keeping things in reserve. She was quite old now, she would tell you, her white head tipped in confidence. She *was* the family. She was pleased to enjoy the china and silver and liked particularly the porcelain dishes with the little pink roses and the gold braid of leaves. I thought my little girl would have loved those, too.

But then the baby died.

Senta set herself to repairing me straightaway. She worked in her kitchen like a mad scientist making me soups, posies, potions. She would not stand by and watch me stumble and weep through the days. She viewed distress as an illness, an imbalance one needed to right. She sent out an All Points Bulletin to her spirit world. The first thing to make its way onto the foyer table, next to a wet vase of fresh flowers and a dish of new berries, was a small brown bottle of Dr. Bach's Emergency Drops. Dr. Bach's drops had once cured Senta's old begonia that had run out of the energy to flower. She took them herself after every sneeze.

I eyed the bottle with cynicism. I had tried it once before, when Senta attempted to cure me of a flu. She held the dropper over my glass of water until she had counted to twenty-six. The taste was awful. The flu survived. I envisioned a letter from Dr. Bach:

*Dear User: Try alcohol or psychotherapy.*

Senta fretted about my being beyond the reach of such extraordinary stuff, but she didn't give up. She copied bits of poetry onto little slips of paper and set them by our mail. Out between the streams of hospital bills, which had a vigorous lifespan of their own, would fall a wisp of paper with Senta's spidery handwriting. Wordsworth. Keats. Whitman. Lines of hope, of renewal, of rebirth. Then, perhaps checking on my progress through this therapy of poets, she would manage to appear whenever I entered the front door. Out of her kitchen, with her apron on and one long thin hand glistening with water, the other poised with a paring knife, she would hail me as though she was consistently surprised to see me still living there.

"I was just thinking of you!" she would shriek gaily. "I was reading the most marvelous book about reincarnation." Then in low conspiratorial tones, "It makes quite a bit of sense, you know. After all, it is only the body that dies. Our souls are left to dance on, until there is another body for us to inhabit. Be happy," she would plead, "you shall meet up with your daughter in another life."

Eventually she gave up on my spiritual salvation and went to work on my body.

"Won't you join me for soup today?" she would shout to me

92

up the stairwell. "I am using an ancient grain, spelt. It is so curative."

At first I boycotted her soups, her cures, but time gradually cauterized the wounds it could not heal, and I grew stronger and more able to reconcile Senta's unmothering love. I would go down to her kitchen with a piece of embroidery and sit at her tiny table and squint at the fabric and prick myself while she put the last touches on her soup. Because at eleven-thirty, or thereabouts, the contents of that quiet buddha of a bowl in the sink was emptied into a pot on the stove and set to boil. Then Senta would begin chopping the carrots, the celeriac, the potatoes, the leeks, all those fresh participants from the market that needed only minutes, not hours, to surrender their flavor and firmness. While they boiled she would slice slivers of brown bread, spread them with soft butter and set them around a small jar of honey. Clover honey. Lavender honey. Chamomile honey. Each destined to rid a particular impurity in the body, my body, which seemed rid of too many things already.

"I have fresh bread for our soup today," Senta would say. "We dine as kings."

Or: "I have put hawthorne berries in my soup today. They are good for the blood."

Or: "If M. would eat my soup he would be a better mayor. But he is a socialist. The world is falling to the socialists."

Senta's soup. It was the axis of the day like a prayer sung on the morning hours, matins, lauds, prime, terse, soup at sext, a nap at nones. It sang of the founding of civilization, the humble origins of mankind, the cultivation of grains, when one woman said to another, "If you soak them for a while in water, they won't break your teeth." And the other woman said, "Oh, thank you. Because we have almost no teeth left. By the way, you can use that extra flour from the mortar to rub on your chest so these hides won't itch so much."

The first conversation. And it took place between women, in a kitchen without walls, and changed the world.

Then Senta's world changed. She fell in love. It was a story riddled with holes, like so many love stories, so that we can go on believing in love and its mysterious trappings the way we believe in folktales of talking trees and the reasoning of fairies. Hua, a thirty-year-old man fresh from mainland China, with scarcely a word of English, found his way over the oceans to the airport of a European city and a university that might accept him—destitute and homeless—into its animal sciences department with a sufficient stipend so that he could find a room and board. He had befriended friends of Senta's at the airport who "saw in him immediately something very special and fine," she said. They gave him some pocket money, and before leaving on a plane themselves they called Senta and asked her to look after him. And so it was that Hua's orange jacket and knapsack of illustrious make were regularly draped over the chair in our foyer. I admired Hua before I met him for turning his fortunes around so sharply.

The Senta I had come to know disappeared, retired to hidden rooms like the good girl who deflects suitors toward her older sisters. No longer did I find her ambling about the house and garden with her white hair wildly awry and a pair of rusty garden shears poised for pruning in a bony hand that had forgotten they were there. No longer did I catch her draped in old shirts from her father's musty closet, with one or two damp kitchen towels slung across her shoulders from soup-making hours ago, a piece of twine about her waist, a rubber band in her pocket for emergencies. Someone else was popping through the doorways downstairs with comely white hair coiffed professionally, someone sporting a silk dress only forty years old, a gold pin at the collar and stockings around her two pencil-thin calves.

She fancied herself aloud to be a grandmother figure to Hua. She found him a room in the house of an acquaintance, where he had a bed and a desk and a place to plug in his rice cooker. He came to Senta's villa every Wednesday afternoon for tea and on Sundays for lunch and a nap.

"Hua is napping," she would whisper to me, a finger to her lips. I'd see his pastel-colored knapsack on the foyer chair. "He always naps on the sofa between three-thirty and five o'clock. He finds it to be quite a critical piece of the day."

Senta believed him to be infinitely delicate and refined. He struck me as a kind of pasha.

"Today he helped me in the garden," she continued, "cutting the dead peach branches. You know, he begins very slowly," she explained with an edge of sharpness, as though confirming one's suspicions that he might be, well, a bit lazy. "But then he completes the task particularly well. With artistry. He does everything so beautifully."

*He helped her in her garden. Her garden was her bed.*

I saw Hua's black head of hair from our balcony, but I didn't meet him for months. Invitations to soup were cut back. New smells echoed from the kitchen, yodeled their way up the stairs so that I might know of changes afoot.

Hua's cultivated palate was the fame that preceded him. Senta worried away her Tuesdays and Saturdays deciding what to cook for him on the following days. It was quite impossible for him to eat meat, and nothing but fresh ingredients would satisfy. There was the issue of how carefully she cut the carrots, because carrots, in Hua's book, were things to be sculpted, not chopped. Fresh bowls of fruit graced Senta's kitchen table now. Bruised brown pears, plums with festering scars, strawberries gone purple, were banished. New teas in captivating boxes appeared on Senta's countertops, diminishing the luster of her old faience spice jars and screaming to be recognized. Moreover, the milkman was coming twice a week, instead of just once, to ensure fresh butter and cream. There had been a regretful incident with a Sunday's pudding.

"Hua is so sensitive," Senta beamed in explanation, a pearl broach on her blue silk breast. "I made him my pudding, his favorite, vanilla. I make it every Sunday for dessert. You know," she murmured a quiet aside, "he really doesn't believe in eating sweets—with only this exception.

"But last Sunday," Senta went on in lower tones, "he simply could not eat the pudding. 'The milk is off,' he said. 'That's impossible,' I said. I said I would certainly have a word with the milkman. And so I did, on Monday . . ."

Having firsthand knowledge of Senta's old refrigerator myself, and having seen the flora and fauna blossom there on the cream, quark, butter, cheese, and milk pitcher, I was apologetic on behalf of the milkman, who could only be expected to deliver fresh milk, but who could not be held responsible for its sequestration.

Hua's presence became a part of our lives in the villa. His English improved. He made great strides at the university. On Sundays he ever-so-slowly pruned Senta's fruit trees, or thinned the wild anemones, or detangled a blackberry vine from the necks of other flowers. Never hard labor. Never the turning of the compost pile. Then he would have his important nap on the sofa. Eventually I met him, and several times thereafter I bumped into him coming and going in the foyer, taking off or donning his admirable jackets. Sometimes he brought his rice cooker and it sat gleaming on Senta's countertop like a landed UFO. He taught her how to whip an egg into her vegetables. Senta said it was a feast for the senses.

"He is a much better cook than I!" Senta exclaimed.

"Oh no," Hua demurred.

Once I bumped into him coming up from the cellar with a big jar of pear preserves. I flushed. I had been with Senta the day she made those preserves, helped gather the brown pears from the gravel and ivy beds where they fell. We had brought buckets into the kitchen, and with them, buckets of fruit flies too drunk and heavy to fly. We had sorted through the pears and peeled them and scooped out the holes made by bird beaks and tunneled after the dim brown spots to find their inhabitants. We had sliced and boiled and sugared the pears as though preparing for a wartime famine. We had boiled the jars and the rubber seals and turned Senta's kitchen into a factory with sweet-smelling refuse, a huge pail of rotting pear flesh and fruit flies for vultures and it was our world.

But there was no war. Only Hua walking off with the spoils, nettling me with his innocence, this companion, grandson, and helper of Senta's. He received pocket money from her on Sundays. He never seemed lacking for necessities.

"He has very little," Senta once communicated in knowing, eyebrow-arching tones, "but he has only the best."

Senta's friends, provoked by her girlish spirit, chided her. "You are in love with him," they would spit.

"They're just jealous," I told Senta. Although, I was a little jealous, too. After all, Hua had captured a fat slice of her affections, and I was among those shuttled aside to make room for him. I was not artful in the garden, not at all deliberate when it came to pruning dead branches from her apple tree, and even less picky when it came to eating her soups and puddings. I marveled to think that this was the man for whom she had waited—so gentlemanly, Senta said, that he hardly touched her when he would kiss her hello on the cheek.

I thought back to the day she was cutting roses and remembering that nice man who had asked her to dance, long ago at a church social, and I took a few crayons to my imagination and gave him a soft voice and a feathery touch. It was during those years that Senta purchased the silk dresses she now wore, watery and luminous, that would have dazzled her then-black hair and thick black eyebrows. I imagined her turning not eighty-eight, but thirty-eight, with her small waist and huge round eyes, shy and watchful from the corner of hundreds of little black-and-white photographs she kept in a cardboard box, standing with her hands clasped at her waist, aware of her duties as a child, as a sister, and as a human being. She had nursed each member of her family through their final infirmities, and now suddenly alone at life's conclusion, she was falling in love. Hua was testing Senta's pledge to her pantheon of gods.

For Senta, who never knew, it didn't matter that Hua was gay. Nor did she ever see in his placid expression that he had gradually come to look upon her as a burden. Soon the day came when Hua was offered a job in a city two hours away, and his fine coats and caps disappeared from the foyer. Senta's gait went unchanged. Her newly freed time was swept up by an old ex-student, a woman whose mother had recently died and who would come by with her car, levering Senta into the front seat like a tangle of frozen branches. There was no time to mourn. After nearly a century of men and women coming and going, Senta let Hua leave his colors in a precious corner of her canvas. There was an egg whipped into her soup now, most days. But Hua was gone.

With reluctance, I made note of the fruit tart that Senta made for Hua on the occasion of his new job. It took all morning to command her old fingers, like claws with age and arthritis, to pit the cherries and slice the lemons paper-thin and whip the custard sufficiently. She left a huge piece of it in the foyer for my husband and me. I could hear her cleaning up in the kitchen when I came in that evening, her stiff hand moving in slow circles across the face of the cake plate. And Hua was the name of a dynasty within Senta's own history, a period contained within the entrance and exit of a young Chinese man.

# Hua's Fruit Tart

## THE PASTRY:

2½ cups flour          Salt
2 egg yolks            ¼ cup ground
½ cup sugar               hazelnuts
1½ sticks butter

Fresh slivers of cherries and paper-thin slices of lemons from Sicily

## FILLING:

1½ cups fresh cream        Grated rind and juice
3 eggs                        of 2 lemons
½ cup sugar                1 tablespoon flour

You must chill the pastry after you make it or it will be impossible to roll out. Press it gently into your tart pan. Be careful not to stress your dough, for it will reward you by snapping back in the oven. Cover your dough with parchment and dried beans and bake for 15 minutes or so, to set it.

Place the fresh fruit across the floor of the tart. Whip up your filling and pour it over the fruit. I had to bake my tart for over half an hour because the fruit was bursting with juices!

"I'm quite slow now," she sighed to me one afternoon, months after Hua had left. She was back into her old clothes and twine, her old brier patch of white hair. The gold brooches had disappeared back into the bank vault, like marvelous shells snatched back by the sea at night. Her feet were troubling her and she was seeing a new pedicurist, who recommended herbal foot baths. "I am just bones with a bit of skin stretched around."

Indeed, Senta was little more than a skeleton for all the years that we knew her. I felt the frailty, the nothingness when I hugged her, and it reminded me of the last time I hugged my mother while she was alive. I had bent over my mother's hospital bed and gently searched for the outline of her shrunken skeleton beneath the white sheets. Then I placed my hands on her arms and lowered my head softly onto the bones of her bosom, which had once been so soft and fragrant, and spoke of my love. I cradled her cool frame with my warm flesh. So I was grateful to hug Senta—not like Hua, the scarcely touching gentleman—and clasp her tight about the shoulders.

"Ah," she said once, sensing the need in my touch. "If life were not so difficult, no one would want to die."

I pulled back and saw her wry smile and felt as though I were looking down a long honeycombed tunnel of years.

"I am very old," she said, aware that I was feeling her frailty. Then she took my face in her hands. "And very young, too."

From my own kitchen window above Senta's, I could see the new woman friend carting Senta off to see the botanical gardens, or to have a picnic, or attend a concert. There was the unbendable Senta, propped, smiling, a figure from another toy set plopped into this toy car. Her eyes were wide with anticipation. She was cheery regardless of those aching feet, the odd pain in her thigh, a bad tooth.

"It is nice to do things, but it is always better to come home," she said to me later as I sat in her kitchen sharing a pot of melissa tea. She would serve me only melissa and chamomile tea now, as I was pregnant again and she was determined to calm my nerves. "Green tea makes the Chinese very tranquil," she said, "but it is not good for babies."

Senta was at her sink, looking out the window with the tall iron stanchions of ivy, the watery vision of her old eyes trained on something beyond the melting panels of old glass. With all those lenses warped in sequence, I wondered what she might see—fractured light, mirages, images that shifted if she advanced. Perhaps one distortion would compensate for another and correct an illusion. Or perhaps she was only looking inside, seeing with the hindmost fragments of her eyes, reminding me that the earth in shadow, unlit by the sun, was also alive. How often I would catch my own mother that way, stilled at the kitchen window as though it were the gateway to some perfumed realm, a private entrance to collapsed memories. So I said nothing to interrupt. The kitchen resonated with the rustle of old images folding gently into new ones.

Senta's teas strove in vain to quench my anxieties through a new pregnancy. By seven months my worries were spilling into all other areas of my life, because no bowl was big enough to hold what loss, that open spigot of anguish, could yield. I began to panic about Senta's health. I left fresh flat rye breads—her favorite—on the foyer table, nurturing her as she was nurturing me with her teas, ensuring that she would be there at the door the next time I came home from the hospital and we could rewrite together that former scene.

As my belly grew, we spoke less and less of our hopes. We erased the thick exuberant tracery that fills the margins of a pregnancy, and we penciled in no gay expectations. In that villa of forces beyond ourselves, neither one of us would bait the ill-will of any god. Senta discreetly invited the hunched woman back to rependulum the rooms. The piano had to be moved one foot to the East, but nothing else. We waited.

"Readiness is all!" she would shout to me from downstairs. "Shakespeare!" she would add, demonstrating to me and to the spirit world alike that she might be deaf but she was no thief of fine lines. "*Hamlet!*"

And then Hugh. Hugh was born on September 7, 1994, and life, which had seemed like a heap of raw wool before—a tumble of brier, filth, and chaos—was suddenly spun gold.

Senta put on a blue silk dress, took her best cane, and hobbled along the sidewalk to the hospital. She came bent, frail, exhausted, and trembling. She carried a posy fresh from her garden, and fresh, too, were the scratches on her translucent hands where a rose had not forgiven her for snipping it. She entered my room surrounded by nurses, some of whom had been her students, some of whom were only concerned for her as she moved in uncertain steps down the hospital corridor. But Senta was beaming.

"I have never seen such a young baby," she said, her aged eyes gazing down upon my sleeping newborn. She refused to hold him. "Germs," she whispered. She would not even sit. "I cannot stay. You need rest."

"Don't go, Senta," I pleaded, allowing myself to say what I could never say before. But she would not stay. She chatted a moment with the nurses in a dialect that twirled by me, charming them with some story I couldn't understand. They giggled, enchanted, and dispersed.

"When will you come home?" she asked. She had paused at the doorway, resting there before the daunting walk back. She was smiling, but a large tear like a Russian jewel stumbled down her very wrinkled cheek. It was a gift, like the fresh water that beaded and chased down her vases, like the small pink petals trapped in her white hair, a part of her poetry that connected all living things.

"Soon," I said.

"You know," Senta said, tipping her head, "the very young and the very old are happiest at home."

Home, beneath the thick and thickening crust of her memories. Home, with those angels that counted Senta among themselves, that helped her stand up after she had been on her knees in the garden, that helped her rise from her bed each stiff morning, that massaged her brittle spine so she might bend to bandage a bleeding shin.

"*Engeli chömed!*" Senta would cry out to the air. "*Angels come!*"

From our rooms above her wilderness, I would hear her call and I would feel the air shiver with the energy of an immense love. Later I would hear her singing while she arranged fresh-cut flowers in the kitchen, and I would know that I was living above a choir of angels, because although I could only hear Senta's voice, it was the sound one voice makes when it is singing in harmony with many.

She gave you the impression that she had already been to heaven, and you may imagine her there, in the center panel of a triptych, her white hair tied back with a rope of flowering clematis. Christ and His apostles have spoons in their hands as they wait for Senta to bring them her soup. For after The Last Supper there might still be Senta's Soup, because it's heaven.

There were as many versions of Senta's Soup as there were passages in her heavy leather Bible, but here is a recipe that she once wrote down for me. The measurements are handfuls, and the eye must guide.

## *Senta's Soup*

| | |
|---|---|
| Barley grains | Leeks |
| Dried chickpeas | Celery |
| Brown or white rice | Potatoes, peeled |
| Wheat berries | Parsley |
| Bulgur | Peppercorns |
| Peas | Bouillon |
| Carrots | |

All sorts of vegetables, important a big carrot, if possible celery, leek, fennel, and some green stuff (put in at the end), all cut fine or grated. Keep all boiling with bouillon. If you want it especially nourishing add some wheat or barley, or spelt, or soy kernels, or rice. Finally a whipped egg improves the soup. No definite measures, let instinct be your shepherd. (I don't use beets for they overrun with their color. I do not care for onions or cabbage.)

Lovely with bread and butter and lavender honey.

Be grateful.

⟶

Some months after Hugh was born, we moved back to America, to our first house, our first two thirds of an acre, and our first fights about mowing a lawn. The homecoming and the home-owning reminded me how much of my life would be built without my mother, and now it would be built without Senta, too. I felt as though my heart were laced with abandoned mining tunnels, and timbers deep within continued to collapse in times of great loneliness.

*March on.*

There were transporting moments: Hugh discovered watermelon; I joined a reading group; I became pregnant again; Hugh discovered sour cream and onion-flavored potato chips; my husband dug grand garden beds out of the sod; Hugh invented walking.

Then Madeleine was born, on March 1, 1996, a second daughter carved from the softest pink marble, whose dark eyes fastened on mine with such conviction that I took her to be a soul reincarnate, eons older than I was, sent here in bone and blood to strengthen me. I would strap her to my back like a battery pack, and we would pursue a toddling Hugh, prowl the supermarket aisles, feel a maple's shade. We would perch on the front yard fence counting cars that drove by—anglers, with our smiles, trawling for companionship. We made a busy trio by day, an exhausted quartet by night.

I telephoned Senta to tell her about Madeleine, but the connection was poor and I had to shout into the receiver until the good news sounded ugly—loud and staccato. I issued a virtual Gulf Stream of photographs across the Atlantic and back came Senta's spidery letters: The garden was a wilderness; she had gone to a concert; she was feeling old.

*I have just had a luncheon,* she wrote, *and now I must nap. People are so complicated. I cannot have complicated visitors anymore.*

My longing to see Senta throbbed like an inflammation. When Maddie was just over one year old, I put the family on an airplane to Zürich. We took a taxi to the villa, which seemed to greet me shyly from within the shadows of ivy, pine trees, and droopy hazelnut branches. If home were a taste, this villa was that flavor on my tongue. But I had no key this time; it was no longer my front door. I rang and knocked, squinting through the thick glass to find her wooden figure listing toward the door.

"Senta!" I cried.

We were a noisy blur beyond the panes. Senta opened the front door and slowly absorbed the scene. There were pruning shears and a branch of browning apple blossoms in her hands. Her white hair had snared many tiny green leaves. My children's eyes were round with wonder. We stared across the threshold for a moment, voiceless, assuring ourselves that the River Styx was not flowing between us.

"Hugh and Madeleine," Senta said slowly. "But I have just been looking at your pictures!"

She embraced me with reserve; the arrival of our bundled exuberance somewhat alarmed her. Then she beckoned us to sit in her garden, where wild strawberries the size of marbles dangled under small spade-shaped leaves. Senta tried to interest the children in hunting for these berries. She showed them a tall fat stalk of asparagus, she offered them vegetable juice and biscuits, but they preferred throwing white gravel from her garden paths. Hugh and Maddie were beyond her enticements. They were melting with fatigue.

"Perhaps they would like my pears?" Senta suggested. I tried to dissuade her but she hurried into the kitchen, where the serenity of the spirit world was breathing densely. Pock! gasped the rubber seal on a jar, cool from the cellar. A serving spoon pinged into the silence as it dished slices and syrup into two porcelain bowls. Senta set a silver teaspoon in each. Then she placed them on cream-colored lace doilies on a beautiful tray, with a tin of whole-meal biscuits besides, but when she returned to the garden, the children in our arms were snoring.

It was as though they didn't mix, Senta and the the babies, two kinds of magic with no wand in common. I saw myself in the middle, always trying to condense and pull together the disparate pieces of my life as though I could create one nugget for my affections, one home for my strongest attachments. It was unconscious, instinctual. Had I stirred it with a spoon, a larger truth would have surfaced: that I sought expressly neither to connect their love nor to simplify mine, but rather to knit more tightly the layers of love around myself, and to leave no holes. *This last one, this fifth, is so needy.*

The next day I met Senta, alone, at the open market. We toured our favorite stalls—the mushroom seller, the couple from Chur with honey, the bearded man who had nice berries. Senta bargained with a woman over a rose. I wanted to buy her more flowers, but she protested that she had too many already. I tried to buy her a rye bread, but she waved me off; there was yet half a loaf in her drawer. I tried to pull her market cart, but she insisted that it served as her cane.

After an hour we paused to rest on the lip of a fountain.

"On Tuesdays there is a woman with roses for a franc," Senta said, still piqued about the price she paid earlier. Her eyes tipped up above me and she sang out,

*"Knowst thou the land where the lemon trees bloom,*
  *Where the gold and orange glows in the deep thicket's gloom*
  *Where a wind ever soft from the blue heaven blows,*
  *And the groves are of laurel and myrtle and rose?"*

She smiled as though a tremendous wing had stirred a pleasing breeze for her. "Goethe." Then her eyes drifted down to mine, and she clasped my hands in her own. "Thank you so much for coming," she said quietly, graciously.

"Senta," I sputtered, words and tears foundering in my throat.

"Don't cry, darling. If we do not meet here again, we shall meet in heaven."

# 4

## *Two in the Kitchen*

WHEN I FIRST SAW my husband chopping green beans into uniform inches, I thought the marriage would never last. It was so precise, so painstaking. It was the way his mother did it. He liked his green beans cut small, but then he went and married a woman who manhandled green beans—no knife, no ruler.

"They're nice this way," he had the nerve to say, chopping carefully.

"Tough," I said sweetly.

My husband will tell you that men have always belonged in the kitchen. Men, in my husband's book, need to examine the steak, prod the steak, sometimes marinate the steak, and then grill the steak. The grill is his kitchen annex, and how lucky to find it out on the patio, beyond the ring of telephones and the wail of crawling babies, or sometimes even further afield, at the threshold of the garage. It is where he disappears to, more regularly on spring nights with a glass of Burgundy in one hand and the grilling fork in the other, but not infrequently on winter nights, in ski jacket and gloves, hovering happily over a spitting grill like a merry pauper warming his hands over a fire of roasting chestnuts. So much is this his terrain that I haven't a clue about grilling myself, even in spite of his repeated and enthusiastic verbal descriptions that begin with a concrete calculation about the amount of charcoal, stacked, and in what configuration, and end with a kind of reverie about instinctive cooking times and a sixth sense for the proper aeration of the coals.

Apart from grilling, my husband gets interested in few cooking projects. He hasn't mentioned green beans for years now. Pancakes, oatmeal, an occasional curry, are meals that lure him into the kitchen around once a month. He uses several mixing bowls, somehow, and quite a few disparate utensils, and finds solace in the image of many boxes and cartons and eggshells lying across the kitchen counters during the apocalyptic procedure. He needs the meal to give himself energy to clean up afterward. I watch him making oatmeal for our children, sitting them on the counter too close to the burner, showing them how pleasingly the lumps of brown sugar melt. I see him brandishing his measuring spoons and lecturing them on what he has tried to impart to me for twelve years.

"Cooking is essentially chemistry."

Sometimes I want to take a can opener to him.

I have to be careful answering. If I likened cooking to art, he would tell me that paints were chemicals, too, and even tell me which chemicals. This would be troublesome news because I prefer to think of paints as gorgeous constellations of atoms, pulled from the prism in a persuasive purity of tint, whereas chemistry is one of those brittle sciences, always threatening death with its glass martini stirrers and steel tongs and wildly noxious bubbling substances with incurable names. Chemistry is not on my Most Favored Nations list.

"Chemists," I replied, "belong primarily in Switzerland, because dispassion in experiments is critical, and the hand pouring drops from a glass beaker must be as steady as an alp. Chemistry is for aspirants to a Nobel Prize with a future of secured anonymity. It belongs behind double doors, on rubber tables, in supreme quiet. None of it informs a proper kitchen."

"Why don't you like chemistry?" he asked, he who once blew up his high school chemistry lab, out of love, not rebellion.

"I have nothing against chemistry," I lied. Let us omit the fact, I might say, that chemistry did not cure my mother, or that chemistry sits like a toxin on the labels of my shampoo and soda pretending to avail itself as information when not one person in a million understands the paragraph of words that might as well be sprayed on crop infestations.

"I like kitchen sciences," I said. "I like when the bloody mary runs up my celery stick. I like when purple pole beans turn green in boiling water. I even like to watch vinegar and baking soda erupt when I attempt to clean a scorched pot. But it's cooking in the kitchen, and chemistry in the laboratory, and that's why cooking and chemistry are two different nouns."

Despite our differences of opinion, usually over process and inconsequential to the flavor of the meal, my husband has always been supportive of my cooking. I applaud him for it. He doesn't need his rice to arrive on a cucumber ferry strewn with scallion confetti, and I've never gone into the kitchen looking for an art review. My table is no oil painting. I do my best with the chunk of time and thoughts that I send into the kitchen with marching orders and no sentimentality. Very rarely do my husband and I come to quarrel over food, and when we do it is courteously oblique and mildly intellectual, so as to remove argument from person and vice versa.

"We all need measurement," he says.

"We don't need measurement in all things," I reply.

"But what you do, which is interesting, is that you measure about half of your ingredients, and the other half you just estimate or throw in without concern as to quantity."

"And?"

"Well, there's no real *and*. There's only the impossibility of making something twice."

"And?"

"Suppose you liked something and wanted to make it again. You couldn't."

"I would come close enough," I say. "If the meal were too exacting, I wouldn't want to make it twice. Too much measuring spoils the process. It removes human involvement. It turns the kitchen into a chemistry lab."

There we were again.

"Where does that leave a recipe?" my husband asks.

"As a launching point. Except for baked goods. Then you have to be careful where you improvise."

"But you give recipes to friends. Do you tell them that you don't follow the recipe yourself, but here it is?"

"Not measuring everything is not the same as not following the recipe. It is a question of exactitude in process. All I'm saying is that too much exactitude jettisons me from the kitchen. Watching you cook is appalling. You spend the first half hour finding all the teaspoons, half teaspoons, and quarter teaspoons that have emigrated to odd drawers and basement shelves over the past several years. Then you stir up a beaker of spice powders. You're always interrupting yourself by going back to check the recipe. It takes forever. It's painful to watch. It's like watching a father put clothes on a baby—it takes two hours and the pants are on backward, which is actually okay for a baby, but anguishing to witness for the mother."

My husband thinks. "But you like my curries."

"I love your curries," I say. "I like them more than mine, but I would never make them."

My husband brings too much energy to the scene, cooks with too much intensity, stirs up the sediment at the bottom of my kitchen's consciousness and makes it muddy. When he is cooking up an El Niño, sending eddies of buttery fumes into the family room, raining oil spots down upon the stovetop, blowing hot air laced with oregano across the living room—when all this is going on, and I, unaccustomed to free time between the hours of five and seven P.M., am kicking stray quilt feathers across a carpet, and kicking myself for piddling away this unexpected gift of time, I think: His science is different than mine. Mine is more the ilk of the football captain, who one day bumped into microbiology and liked it, and brought all his unadulterated pleasure and football metaphors to bear upon the laboratory, and made wonderful discoveries. My husband's kitchen has rules, and there is chemistry. Measurement is a balm. Recipes are gospel. Merriment slides down the sink pipes with a last splash and gurgle.

"You cook like your father," my husband will say to me. It sounds like a summation, but he's dying to have me pry it open. I envision the state of his mind: business lunch, shrimp in his vichyssoise, nouvelle catastrophe. But my husband enjoys my father's improvisational cooking. He knows my father is incapable of making a simple hamburger and he takes pleasure in the unconventional menus that issue from my father's kitchen. So I rise to the bait like a dumb trout.

"Meaning?" I smile.

"Why own cookbooks?" He's pleased with this.

"Inspiration," I say. "They act as a foil. They create a kind of dialogue for the lonesome cook." My eyes arch. My father uses cookbooks as paperweights. He uses them as trivets. None of my sisters will even give my father a recipe anymore, because he won't follow it. Then he'll tell you he *improved* it.

"Do you know," my father says now, visiting, "if you just stir a little flour into the sour cream it won't curdle in a boil?"

Hrrrrumph, I think.

"Do you like sautéed mushrooms?" he asks. "Because I have been trying for years to find a good way to do them, and I finally succeeded, with oil, butter, herbs de provence, red vermouth, and a good squish of lemon."

"That's it?"

"That's it," he says. "Oh well, salt and pepper of course."

"That's it?"

"You don't need a lot of vermouth really."

"That's it?"

"It's easy."

He isn't even making his mushrooms at the moment, just thinking about them. He is making a lamb stew. I watch him cut the shoulder steaks into pieces. He's handy with a knife. I see him brown the pieces before sautéing the onion—*before*—and I realize it might well be that Day Three and Day Four in the Old Testament were reversed by a scribe's error. He hums as he minces lemon rind and throws it into the pot, saving a small curl for his martini.

"I've been working on a good mushroom recipe for years," he reflects.

"Ho hum," I say, pushing my toe against the baseboards. This is going on, after all, in *my* kitchen. My father, Grandpa, like some visiting chef.

"So many noodles?" he asks, as I dump a bag headfirst into a pot of boiling water.

"I like cold noodles," I frown. I rest my elbows on the countertop, pouty as a model in a raincoat ad.

He shrugs. "To Each His Own" flickers across his forehead like the Times Square tickertape. When he was a little boy, his mother told him that his lies would be written across his forehead. After mischief, he would walk into a room with a hand clapped across his brow. My father had a mother who didn't protect him from anything, including herself. Especially herself.

He pours his martini while the onions crackle. He chooses a wooden spoon from the pitcher with the pleasure that comes from hours of using one, like a writer holding a pen, teaming up in silence for fulfilling results.

"You don't have to slice the mushrooms," he says. This is considerable propaganda.

I watch my father sashay between cutting board and oven in a comfortable old three-step. In 1944, he survived on K rations and C rations for weeks on the coast of Normandy. Now he reminds me that cooking is either necessary, because otherwise you starve, or cooking is love, because you care.

## Grandpa's Sautéed Mushrooms*

Olive oil                    Red vermouth (3)
Butter                       Lemon wedge (2)
Mushrooms (1)                Salt and pepper
Herbes de Provence

Heat oil and butter in a skillet until very hot. Add mushrooms, herbes de Provence, red vermouth (not too much), and a squish of lemon. Salt and pepper to taste.

Footnotes by the Editor and Daughter, who should know:

1. You need a couple of packages of mushrooms because they shrink.
2. Use half a lemon. He does.
3. Don't even think white vermouth will substitute, he said.

*If you have a cholesterol problem, don't tell your doctor about this recipe. And especially don't tell him you went to the Lobster Shack last weekend for fried clams.

Since there was to be no Grandma on our side, my sisters and I, with our children, threw ourselves like raging floodwaters onto our father, shaping his banks, eroding his solitude, running him over with the force of our needs until he began to resemble a proper riverbed. He moved from Northampton, making a new home nearer to two of my sisters. There, he taught his grand-children how to play poker, first for pennies and then for the house. When the grandchildren started beating him regularly, he taught them how to cheat. He baby-sat. He ate pizza and lo mein and watched horrible movies. He grouted unimaginable gaps for all of us. He took on pieces of my mother's role, and one of those pieces was the kitchen.

If you give my father a recipe and he doesn't follow it, you mustn't let your feelings be scorched. Recipes intrigue him, as they are the Written Word. He looks fresh at them because he didn't spend his life cooking daily for a large family. He has no prejudices about using a bit of salsa in his soups, or putting a dollop of Jamaican burnt sugar in his chili.

"Just don't tell me," I say to him about his ingredients.

He is a renegade in the kitchen, not for the sake of defiance but because he had no formal training; there are no Julia-Child-James-Beard rules. He is retired, and the kitchen is where he passes much creative time. There is no hint of his mother's hearth re-created there, because childhood was not a happy time for him. When he is in his kitchen, he is burying the past.

It was only a short time that my life intersected with that of my father's mother, Sadie, or passed through it like a strand of yarn purled through a loop of its past. She was living on Gramatan Avenue in Mount Vernon, New York, in one of the tall brick apartment buildings that lined the street like parked cars. There are places that hammer history into lead, so that no one finally cares if two Indians bartered away Manhattan for a sack of broken shells, because whatever stands today is so rid of interesting aspect, so bleached of spirit, so deprived of life, that if it were paved over tomorrow it might finally rest in peace as a vacant lot.

Gramatan Avenue seemed like such a place. My brother and sisters and I were infrequently marched into the bowels of Sadie's building, as though into the basement of a hospital—solemnly, somehow naked without the happy wrapping of stories that parents pass on to their children to make their grandparents seem miraculous.

My mother would have had a week of anxiety leading up to these trips. A week of polishing little shoes, of replacing buttons on proper coats, of collecting gradually and silently a trove of laptoys and coloring books and crossword puzzles and nesting them all in the backseat of the station wagon like a marvelous tideline. My father would spend the drive to Mount Vernon with his jaw set and his humor dwindling until it exited for good at the Merritt Parkway, Exit 28, while we sat in the car, stuffed into white socks and Maryjanes and woolen coats, and sang until he snapped at us. Then we whispered and giggled until any sound from us at all threatened to put him on the breakdown lane.

*When I was a little boy*, my father never said to us, as though any of his stories would have been like an iron wrench hurled with fury at the Pietà. He wanted us to form our own image of Sadie, unscarred by his memories, although his withdrawal

119

from the picture would be indictment enough. He removed himself from the board, like a chess piece whisked away, so that we might see his mother straight on and say "Check" by ourselves.

Of course, my mother might have said, *"When your father was a little boy . . ."* but even she never crossed that line into fiction to swaddle her children with a felicitous sense of linkage to their history. Instead, she and my father washed their hands of it all at the altar on June 16, 1949, and made a pledge to rescue each other from their parents and from the pain of their youth and to sculpt for themselves some small community of love and decency and honesty—whatever that was. They did tell us about Aaron, my father's father, who trained first as an electrician and then as a dentist, and who died too young to know his grandchildren. Aaron, whose birthday was my own, became in my childhood's history the unfortunate hero who married the crazy Sarah Gibbs after his first fiancée died from influenza.

On the trip to Mount Vernon we would hear grumblings from the front seat of the car about those Gibbs sisters, May, Betty, Helen, Sadie, Molly, and Bella. There had been boys, too—Louis, Edward, Nathan, Harry, Joe, and David, but it seemed they had behaved themselves, unlike their illustrious sisters. Well, but Helen had married Billy, and Uncle Billy had adored my father and his love was like a life preserver thrown to a little boy drowning in the Gibbs sea.

I sniffed the notorious Gibbs world when we walked into Sadie's small, squared apartment on the corner of the fifth floor, up the elevator and down the corridor and through the door into her world of silver iced-tea stirrers and glass iced-tea stirrers and tiny framed photographs of family that hung like apples from a frame tree. Geegaws, my father called them—the cute frames, porcelain figurines, and silver curlicues that crowned every surface, from the fireplace mantel to the bedside tables to the television set. Every horizontal surface was a little meadow in which knickknacks grazed.

When we arrived for our special visits, the kitchen table and gasp of countertop were buried under white cardboard boxes from the delicatessen. We'd help Sadie find crystal serving dishes for pickled herring and chopped liver, a silver plate to lay out the rye bread and smoked salmon. But it was she who made the butter curls, with a small curved knife that she skidded across the slab of yellow butter. She placed the curls on a bed of ice cubes in a crystal dish.

Sadie's kitchen had a window that looked out to the rear of the building and framed a universe of fire escapes. Her appliances were white and bulbous, made in the era of rounded shapes as though they had been not soldered but inflated. Such was the shape of my grandmother, too, rounded, maybe even soft if she hadn't been wrapped in an armor of underclothes and overclothes with a thousand hooks and eyes.

"Did you love the way she cooked?" I once asked my father.

"No," he said quickly. Then, "Sadie could make a delicious roast beef," he added, without inflection.

She had been cruel to him, her second son, and there was no way to rescind that experience, no mythological reversal by a remorseful god. The history of a mother and her son lay like lead in their laps, and no alchemy could etch or draw from it a prettier story. My father became a psychoanalyst and gave to his patients the compassion and dignity that had been withheld from him for so long.

"There were those cookies," I said. "Mama made them for you."

"The rolled cookies with raisins and nuts." He remembered them, sliced into scrolls or pinched into horns, glazed with jam.

From the shards of information that Sadie supplied, Cynthia had tried to bake those cookies, but it was a difficult task because Sadie came from an era in which a woman's recipes stood for a portion of her worth, and so she lied about them a bit, or a lot, ensuring that her name alone would be tied to their perfection. I imagined her gathering the ingredients in crafty increments over the week, then drawing the shade on the kitchen window and baking them in utter solitude.

It had driven my mother crazy trying to duplicate those cookies from Sadie's porous instructions. It was the era, and it was the Gibbs sisters, and it was Sadie. The truth wasn't of much use to her, and lies were an integral part of her language, and if you graphed her sentences on the chalk board you would see fat fissures in the lines because those lies sat like censors between her cortex and her mouth, laughing, editing, expunging, reinventing; and so entrenched were those fabrications that went on with the wig in the morning and maybe even twisted round her dreams at night, that when my father took her to the emergency room one day she gave her age as fifty-five.

"That can't be, Sadie," my father said. "I'm fifty and you're over twenty years older than I am."

"That was years ago," Sadie said.

As much as stories of Sadie kept her grandchildren giggling through the years, it was a humor fraught with sadness, a circus in which a clown is gored, because she had raised two boys in a house of inventions and betrayals, had cheated them out of the fairytales in which the mother loves beyond herself, promises, protects. Instead, she dressed herself each morning as if girding for battle, in rose-colored gold and heavy brocade dresses and heavier girdles, ringing round her neck ornate timepieces with hidden compartments for small photographs of staring faces, Gibbs faces, Gibbs sisters, impervious to truth.

"Come in and have something to eat," Sadie would say to my father. "You look terrible."

These are the cookies that my father loved, as pieced together by my mother, a kitchen archaeologist. When you give one to your child, hold him or her tight, and crush the misery of a little boy long ago.

# Sadie's Cookies

DOUGH:

4 cups flour
½ teaspoon salt
¼ pound butter

4 egg yolks
½ pint sour cream

FILLING:

½ pound chopped
  walnuts
1½ cups sugar

1 teaspoon cinnamon
1 pound raisins
Grated lemon and
  orange rind

Mix flour, salt, and butter through fingers. Add in yolks with sour cream. Work into dough with hands. Refrigerate overnight (may freeze).

Roll out dough. Sprinkle filling to cover. Roll up into log and slice into ½-inch circles or roll up into several small logs and slice into 3-inch pieces to form horns. Egg white wash or spread jam thinly on top. Moderate oven.

The cookies are done when they're slightly burned, the dough sepia, and the sugar caramelized to black. That's not the kind of instruction anyone wants to copy down on a recipe card.

When I was a child I couldn't understand the fuss about these cookies that crumbled all over your lap and then epoxied your teeth. But I remember my father almost sighing when he came home to a big round tin from Sadie, or later, my mother. The cookies were packed individually in small squares of wax paper. If you were tall enough to open the freezer, you could look in and see the merry-colored tins angled on top of frozen roasts and opened only on occasions, the cookies thawed and meted out like gold pieces. My mother would give us something else if we begged for one. She told us they weren't for children, and they were slightly burned. Sadie's cookies. She burned my father, too.

# 5

## *Ida*

WHEN WE RETURNED to America from Switzerland, my children became emissaries, bridge builders, determined to fill *their* New World with friends and family. They would have preferred standing-room-only in the living room, just as Maddie arranged crowded powwows of stuffed animals in her crib. So I was always on the prowl for freelance aunts and uncles, because I knew that part of my role as mother was to construct, to invent, extended family for all of us. With Hugh as my scout and Maddie as my quiver, I went hunting. Early on we netted Ida, somebody else's mother, somebody else's grandmother. I met her in my reading group, and we adopted her.

"It is normally neurotic to have substitutes," Ida would say. "What do you do if you are halfway into a cranberry bread and run out of white sugar? Well you substitute, of course. Lots of things are sweet."

She would invite me to keep her company as she made her hamentaschen, or her notorious prunes in port, which wanted two cups of port in just the preliminary soaking; or she would call to say I must witness her strawberry bush in bloom, or the speckled species of lilac she could smell from her kitchen sink.

"And bring your marvels," she would add.

I loved to sit at Ida's kitchen table while she cooked and talked, and it might have been easier without the marvels, without the constant apprehension about four little hands rummaging her rooms for breakables; only it wouldn't have re-created the ancient tradition of daughters and granddaughters and infants at the feet of elders, the world's waterfall of women, splashing onto the rocks of one generation after the other; and while the older women busied their hands with flour and egg, chanting meaningful stories of the past, the younger mothers would sit with their eyes orbiting their heads like the moons of Saturn, their eyelids defying gravity, vigilant as the gods of the hearth, because it was the nature of a child to break and get broken, and it was the obligation of the mother to minimize those occasions.

If it had not been Ida's kitchen, it would have been another's. Like the second rush hour of a village, the one after the paid professionals leave for their workplaces and the babies' bellies are full, those women who are left behind make a hive of their scattered houses and fly to the other's back steps across the crush of a gravel path or dewy grass, tapping at the panes of the kitchen door, as though they had endured the night with breath held, dreamed of morning, woken to the cries of infants, counted the minutes to a decent hour, and then flung themselves into the kitchen of a friend, to link, find comfort, come together in the way two beads of water, so independently formed, couple suddenly and become one, a little dome. Women, whose lives are so superimposed, can focus with alarming clarity to show one identical image of life; and so they become something larger, inextricable, as they sip hot coffee at the kitchen table. One chops celery, the other nurses an infant; and their connection defies the laws of physics as though they were one in this stage of their lives, sisters, twins, sensing the world through like antennae, ratifying their experiences for one another.

On the day before Passover, we came in through Ida's back door, mother plus two marvels, clomping and rustling and bumping enough to suggest a circus crew, past the washer and dryer and on into the kitchen, which opened off the hallway to welcome us. I undid our bundles, pitched camp with diapers, bottles, crackers, juice, enough for two toddlers times two hours equals . . . the same as five children dry and fed through a weekend. We beat Ida into her kitchen and flipped on the lights (Hugh), and pulled from Ida's open wall cupboards a glass or ten for juice (Maddie), and listened for the engine of her electric elevator chair to rev up.

Plump and regal, Ida was borne down the staircase on an electric chair-lift. Her arms were crossed over a simple wooden cane and she was perfectly still, waiting or thinking. She seemed to be sitting for a portrait. Maddie, Hugh, and I waited below like a proper audience.

At the foot of the stairs Ida lifted her cane upward to command attention.

"Do you suppose the brain ever rests?" she interrogated herself.

A lilac bruise across the bridge of her nose was the remnant of a fall in her meadow, lumpy with grasses. Her skin was translucent and there was a whiteness to it woven together, it seemed, by the faint purple threads of fairies. She drew a silver necklace with moonstones from her dress pocket, clasped it around her neck and became silvery. White-haired, slow and solemn, she trod on thick soles across the Persian carpet of the foyer and into the granite kitchen, recently renovated as kitchens can be and bodies can't. Ida paused to tug at her stockings the color of Persian-carpet-eating moths and thick, designed to ease the swelling of the dark purple veins in her legs.

"I hate these stockings," she said simply. "They are so undignified. They are uncomfortable and ugly. Why is it so many unpleasant words begin with U? Joseph Brodsky suggested we replace the word *egg* with the letter O. I suggested that we replace all things negative with the letter U. We would avert a lot of confusion if we could simplify our distastes, distill dislike to pure dislike, and forget about the gradations. What do you think?"

I plunked Madeleine on the kitchen floor with some spoons and measuring cups. Hugh was investigating the physical properties of Ida's piano keys.

"I like gradations," I replied.

"Ha! You are right. I like gradations, too."

She moved to and through her kitchen as one for whom familiarity and pattern provided pleasure. She had woken up and come down those stairs and crisscrossed the Sarouk-covered foyer into the kitchen for fifty years. She had repeated this route as a mother raising four children, as a student of psychology, as a widow, and now as a ninety-three-year-old woman whose body was beginning to call a few shots. When I looked again at the stretch of floor from foot of staircase to kitchen counter, I imagined a path in the woods, cleared of its flora, teased at knee-height by the brushy leaves of insistent ferns and smooth as planed mahogany from years of tribal feet bustling back and forth, for berries and roots, back and forth, from mortar to pot.

"Without gradations, you truncate life," she continued.

"Ida, I sometimes think I would enjoy a truncated life. I mean, truncated in certain sensitivities."

Ida laughed at me.

"The young want all," she said, "until they can decide what they want. *Swings the cradle back and forth*," she sang in a fluty voice.

Ida had been taking singing lessons once a week at the piano, which was at the moment under Hugh's wrecking-ball fists.

"When you get to be my age," Ida said, "and not everyone does!—you see that a truncated life is not to be envied at all. How boring! What a waste of years! Muddling through with only a dull sense of direction, only a funny thumping sound in the bush to mark your emotions. How are you, people ask, and all you can say is, okay, so-so, blah-blah-blah."

Ida peered down at Maddie. Kitchen implements were splayed in a ring around her as though a centrifugal force based in her spine had sent them spinning. Under Ida's silvery attention, Maddie smiled and squealed and her little body squirmed in recognition of her proud industry.

"Your mama is a coward," she grinned at the baby. "And you are a flirt!"

Ida veered over to a place of switches. It was a kitchen corner complete with desk, telephone, answering machine, filing cabinet, light switches, fan switches, house alarm panel—all these bold green and red buttons awaiting the touch of antique fingers that were born in Boston almost a century ago under the glimmer of gaslight. To the right was a wall of built-in shelves with a stereo system and a bank of cookbooks mixed with mugs, saucers, and knickknacks. It seemed incongruous with my image of Ida as a highly intellectual matriarch that she allowed bits of kitsch to infiltrate her house—a tiny flowery book on kittens, a ceramic pumpkin, a little frame with babies in cartoon. Ida would have said that my snobbery painted me as young; she might even have said that youth was my jailer, jailing me in my narrows, jailing her in my limited image of her. She would have said that if I were so lucky as to make it to ninety-three, I would be less exacting in my tastes. I might have great-great-grandchildren, who would give me birthday presents, like ceramic pumpkins, that seemed marvelous to them. I might have a cat in my history that would change my feelings about the drugstore-quality deification of cats.

A large mural of a receding road, tree-lined and almost sunny, rose up in Ida's corner of desk and switches. It was painted by her eldest daughter, Miriam, half a century ago. Something in the colors was stubborn and refused to be gay. Ida once told me that Miriam refused to be merry, or she was incapable of it, from the moment she was born.

"She wouldn't eat," Ida said suddenly. "Miriam, I mean. My first baby and she wouldn't eat. Oh! Do you know how distressing that was? For a woman to give birth to an unhappy baby . . . it was terribly hard. Sometimes at five in the afternoon, after a long day of managing her discomforts, I would lie her on a blanket on the floor and play Brahms or Mozart. She was quiet then. Miriam loved music. It gave her spatial dimension. Mozart gave her peace. She didn't want anything that I had to give her."

Ida paused. "Miriam is nearly seventy now, and she has Parkinson's disease. My husband gave her that. He was a world-famous brain surgeon, you know. Miriam is so gallant."

Her hands were arrested in the air above her desk like a conductor with his baton up, and stilled, to hush the theater. But she seemed to have forgotten what she was looking for, which switch was still without a flip. Ida was in the middle of Miriam's road, Miriam's vision, a paralyzed landscape almost ugly in its determination to avoid easy prettiness, and it waylaid her immediate purpose.

"Did you read yesterday's science section?" Ida continued. "They've discovered that genes determine if you are a happy person or not. Isn't it fascinating! Not that you can't help a sad baby find some pleasure, and not that you can't render a happy baby senseless with the proper amount of abuse . . . Miriam is brilliant. But she is encased in her Parkinson's now. My husband said to me once, 'Ida, it mummifies, I am being buried alive inside.' "

Staring down the road that Miriam as a child painted in the corner to make it not a corner, Ida sat and listened to the messages on her answering machine. They filled the kitchen like voices from the past, chipping the air like wayward specters. Ida held court in her kitchen, to the voices, to the memories, to visitors, held court like a proper queen, her movements minimal, the movement of people around her like the mad looping of bees.

While Ida listened to her voices, Maddie crawled toward her cupboards. A kitchen is a kitchen is a kitchen, I imagined her humming to herself. I looked into the hallway to find Hugh at the top of the stairs with one of Ida's canes. He had carefully pulled it up alongside himself in order to drop it through the banister railing. It is the role of the mother of toddlers always to be catching them on the brink of some grand auto-da-fé, or sometimes just after it. I offered him several things from my shoulder bag instead of the cane, and he graciously allowed me to distract him. Down plummeted keys, wallet, notebook, a paper bag with half a bagel inside. Bingo. He knew that bag. Throwing himself onto his belly, he surfed down the stairs to retrieve it. I fixed him a place at Ida's table to finish his bagel with some juice. Still at her desk, Ida turned and watched him intently.

"Man creates harmony from the balances and imbalances of his universe," she said. "Or should I say, woman creates harmony from the balances and imbalances of her universe. Few men seek out harmony. They leave themselves with jutting forms. Miriam has her harmony, although she has had little peace in her life. But then, peace is for few. You need a strong ego for peace, and only four percent of the whole population has a strong ego. I was born with a very strong ego," she added.

"What does that mean?"

"It means I don't recognize insult," she laughed. "Ha!"

A sure finger, bent and white, reached out to the radio as God reached out to Adam and gave it voice. She was like a god of the marble age, her white skin veined in lilac.

The kitchen filled with the busied notes of a Beethoven piano concerto. Hugh, bagel in one hand and juice cup cradled to his chest, skipped off to the piano again. He was evidently moved to slap away at the keyboard one more time. Harmony, I mused, as per the important paws of a toddler. If our spirits were unhobbled by our frailties when we died, then we would need an eternity to accomplish all we had been forced to defer in life. I would sit on a cloud with my family around me and my first baby, for eternity a baby, in my lap as I knitted her sweaters forever, while Beethoven grumbled to a music critic on the next cloud over, "Actually, I did hear the canons at the gates of Vienna, but I was desperate to finish a coda."

"I shall bake a cake today to rid the house of flour," Ida said. "My brain has been wondering what flavor. It is sifting the air for inspiration. Well, since Beethoven is accompanying us this morning, I shall bake a linzertorte that is complicated and heavy. And to bow to the spirits of healthiness, I shall use marg instead of butter. Don't tell."

I wondered whether the linzertorte had crowded out the plan for chicken soup with matzo balls, the way a Beethoven symphony could overwhelm a Yiddish folk song. But Ida had to make that soup. It was assigned to her for the feminist seder she was hosting, and we were here to learn Ida's mother's recipe for chicken soup that was Famous, she said. And because Ida was one of those people to whom I enjoyed listening, to whom I posed very few questions, I took Famous as Famous and didn't worry much about the word or its truth or its fiction. I was there to keep her company, for soups take time, and to soak up Ida, her thoughts, her calm, and humor, her love of my children, and her portrayal of the silvery smiling grandmother giving more spoons to Maddie Spoon-Monger. Whether it was linzertorte or seder soup or just two hours with Ida over breakfast, it was two hours with Ida, my Ida, Grandma Ida, in her kitchen.

She toasted bread for her breakfast and spooned cottage cheese onto the plate. I remembered my mother's love of toasted rye bread and cottage cheese, her love of routine, the same simple meal at noon, or late morning, that would allow her to sustain a continuum; so that nothing would deflect her thoughts from some awkward sentence in her book, so that she could stay on the scent of Kant, and not lose it in a rainfall of options for lunch. Nor did she cater to the whims of five hungry children at midday, but rather supplied sandwiches which were to be eaten—no negotiations about bread and fillings. Indeed, if anything were to puncture the serenity of chewing mouths it might be our mother suggesting we reflect on Vietnam, where helicopters and not sandwiches were landing on kitchen tables. Fewer queries, fewer dialogues in that house of nonstop conversation, so that she could repeat new French vocabulary while she spread tuna fish across ten open slices of square bread and think up characters' names while setting two cookies on the edge of each plate and jot a note on a pad while five strong jaws set themselves to the work of chewing and—my God—not talking.

My mother decried the easy trap of restaurants—no fuss, no dirty dishes—because they were dens of interruption. There wasn't time to think through a short sentence at a restaurant table before some waiter would come and ask how things were going? something else? swish! went the check and then you were out the door and weeping on the pavement, exhausted from maintaining a minimum of decorum with five overexcited children and poor food and too many straws and sugar packets that were Not Toys. She felt both children and adults needed to find peaceful interludes in their days to restore the spirit in a world of deafening noise. In our house, lunch at the kitchen table was such a time, because at dinner the father presided and courteous conversation might be conducted over a meal. My mother insisted on tranquil hours in the big yellow house, even if tranquil meant a zipped mouth after a harsh scolding, so that her small community could catch its communal breath. She also laid out quiet places in the house, and the kitchen was one of them, where children might be but could not call attention to themselves. The organic energy constellated in children's bodies could explode its stars in children's rooms, or even better, in the basement, or even *better*, outside.

But where was I? My thoughts, like parcels wrapped in my mother's kitchen, fell from the delivery truck with a thud into Ida's kitchen. Hugh's Ping-Pong assault on Ida's piano was making a crescendo into forte. He had woken me up to my life as it was now, not the child but the mother of.

"Hugh is playing Philip Glass," I said. There was apology in my voice for bringing cacophony to Ida's peaceful house so early in the day.

"Hugh is composing," Ida said. She poured herself a teaspoon of blackstrap molasses and downed it without a grimace. "Men always compose that way, boldly, aggressively. They take whacks at life. Men," she swung toward me, "don't like gradations."

"That must make your practice interesting," I smiled. Ida was—
still at ninety-three—a marital therapist. Only a few months ago
she had cut back to eleven hours a week, conceding to her body's
need for rest, a moratorium on full-time employment. It was a
unilateral demand. Unilateral demands offended Ida, except
when she made them.

"I feel sympathy for the man in a marriage today," she continued, "because he is so without resources, so without options, so
without a clue. Where is my tea strainer?"

"My mother used to say that women had to bring men along."

"Today they don't *have* to. That's what should worry men. Ah,
here is my strainer. Madeleine was eating it. You may have a
slotted spoon, dear, instead."

"I sometimes wonder if women will marry men in the future,
Ida."

"We will. Do you want the Darwinian explanation or the more
complicated explanation? I nearly said the Freudian explanation,
but I caught myself. Thank God. Freud said a woman's anatomy
is her destiny." Ida paused. "I could kill him for that. And penis
envy? Ha! How absurd."

Ida became a feminist when it took courage to be a feminist.
She founded centers for divorced women, she founded programs
for women seeking to return to work after decades of motherhood.
She marched into church basements for feminist meetings while
men stood outside calling her a castrating bitch. And here in
Ida's own kitchen she tended to a stream of women whose marriages were sagging under the weight of feminism or resentment
or misunderstanding or abuse. I looked at the bentwood chair
beside mine and imagined them, one by one, their backs curved

into question marks as they rested their heads upon her little round table and sobbed. He has left me. I have left him. He beats me. He ignores me. He loves someone else. I love someone else. He won't let me be a mother. He abuses me. And now I have the responsibility to say no. I want marriage to beckon and pull at me, the way passion once did. I am afraid when single motherhood seems to call—a wolf's far-off howl in the black night.

Ida had seen the whole internal ruckus of countless private lives bubble over onto her kitchen floor. It was hardwood gone wavy from years of traffic and tears. Ida handled many ruckuses and finally she went back to school so that she could handle them professionally. Suddenly she was getting paid to handle them. She was guiding the ruckus and tears into her office off the foyer and leaving the kitchen floor to flour dust and fruit bits.

She made tea. She did it in silence, ensconced in a purpose and familiarity that removed her from her surroundings and circumstance. She sank into her kitchen surround like a figure in a Cezanne painting that was connected physically, by paint, with another figure, but was completely disconnected in spirit. Ida was apt to depart at times. She would do it without apology, but she would always come back. She would usually come back. Today she came back. She set a cup of tea in front of me.

"Women and men are not equal. They are complementary." Ida lowered herself into a chair beside me. She had a box of matzo meal in her hand. It looked as though the soup would reveal itself after all. "The recipe on the back of the box is not bad, but it isn't as good as mine. You want a matzo ball that lends flavor to the soup, and soaks up the soup's flavor. All at once. Giving and receiving. Like lovers."

"Men and women seem to spend their lives trying to understand each other," I said.

"Oh, men don't. Men rarely even try to understand themselves."

"I find myself in a rage, sometimes, when I expect my husband to do something, or understand something, the way a woman would. It's a quirky trap and I fall into it periodically. We fight and fight and fight, and I think, this is it, it's over, I can't stand the fighting. And then we soften, or crack under the burden of it. Sometimes I wish we could be that couple that races through the fight during the day and makes up in bed that night. It sounds so tidy."

"Doesn't happen," Ida said.

"People say . . ."

"People like to believe."

"People tell you—"

"People like to talk," said Ida. She peered again at her box of matzo. "You need chicken fat to make this marvelous, and nutmeg. Nutmeg is the secret."

She took a pencil to the recipe on the box and revised it, and this is Ida's recipe:

## *Ida's Matzos Kloese (Dumplings)*

| | |
|---|---|
| 1 cup boiling water | 1 teaspoon salt |
| 1 cup matzo meal | Pepper and nutmeg |
| 2 tablespoons chicken | to taste |
| fat or butter | ½ teaspoon dried |
| 1 egg | parsley |

Pour boiling water over matzo meal, stir until water is absorbed, add fat, then egg, seasoning, and parsley. Mix well. Place in icebox, and let stand 1 hour or longer. Roll dough into balls the size of a walnut. If sticky, grease palms of hands or moisten with cold water occasionally. Drop into boiling soup 15 minutes before serving. Boil gently uncovered.

"Don't stint on the nutmeg," Ida said. She underlined it.

~

My tea was weak. I liked having old tea from Ida's dusty boxes in her kitchen. I enjoyed at her table a modest range of tastes: instant coffee, old bread, milk mixed up from powder. She was a break from the fanatical hunt for flavor that marked modernity. I reflected on my own kitchen cupboards and their fancy bottles of oil and vinegar, the espresso beans kept fresher in my freezer, the nectarines tossed into the bin when they looked too tired. Ida's staples were practical, bland, satisfying, and simple. A tired nectarine had a home in her kitchen, until it proved itself rotten. Her days of hunting down the trendy items were over.

Ida finished her toast with cottage cheese and moved toward the kitchen counters to begin her matzo balls. She said, "Women need to have more compassion for men in a marriage. And it's just not fair. But," she added slowly, "it's life."

"I'm surprised by friends who see marriage as some kind of fifty-fifty partnership."

"Well, it should be a partnership. What do you tell them?"

"I tell them nothing—Nothing—is fifty-fifty in a marriage."

"What do they say to that?" Ida smiled.

"Some tell me I'm old-fashioned. Others are grateful. I'm rarely outspoken about marriages in general, but this fifty-fifty stuff is bad propaganda."

Ida said, "What are you going to tell Madeleine about marriage?"

I looked at this little baby with her father's very long eyelashes. She was batting them at us while chewing on a colander. Madeleine had a long torso, plump as a dahlia bulb, and legs slightly bowed. Her feet were small and thin, thinner at least than her brother's feet, which were square. With her little mews and the way she would throw a ballerina's hand across her eyes to sleep, she had been teaching me how different the female was from the male. I knew better what her adolescent years would be like than Hugh's, and I worried for her, because the ascents and descents seemed steeper for girls these days and the fun seemed to be over earlier. And look, there we were, three generations of women in Ida's kitchen while Hugh had marched off to build, investigate, amuse, undo.

"One thing I need to do," I said, "is let Maddie know that marriage and children don't necessarily rule out graduate degrees. I came to motherhood unprepared. I was sent out to educate myself, and come what may on the family side."

Ida laughed. "That's because your mother was one of those feminists who had to fight for her opportunities, and those opportunities fell, plop, into your lap just as they will into Madeleine's lap. You have the luxury to tell her that having a family and a career can be braided. In my youth, a girl was only told how to be a good wife and mother."

Ida began to assemble her ingredients. Stepping over Madeleine, she found a steel mixing bowl and set it on the granite with a whank. Her kitchen had old wood floors and spanking new granite countertops and together they said, "This is me and that's me, too." Like Ida, both tender and tough.

"Ida," I said. "If marriage were reduced to a letter, which would it be?"

"Good question!" she hurrahed, the queen granting knightship for wit.

Ida was doubling the recipe, because twenty-four women were coming to her feminist seder this year. She measured two cups of matzo meal and set two cups of water to boil. ("Goose fat is divine, but bad for the heart.") She set out her eggs and seasoning. When the water boiled, she raised the pot with two hands and poured it carefully onto the dry white dune. Her ninety-second year had been a bad one, she said to me once, because she had felt so let down and defeated by her body. Now, at ninety-three, she had made peace with the trembling, the fragility, and sudden giving out. She used two hands for hot things in the kitchen, two hands for hot coffee, two hands to steady a pot off the stove. It humiliated her, she said, but then, ninety-three years wasn't bad for a body.

She wrapped her knotty fingers around a spoon and stirred the matzo meal. She cracked two eggs into a bowl and tossed in the seasoning without measuring. My mother taught me to make things from scratch. Boxes were harder, she felt, and the results were horrible and artificial, whereas after you baked or cooked from scratch a few times, your hands remembered everything and you never had to read the recipe again. You were on automatic pilot, your mind free to explore the skies.

"X," Ida finally exclaimed, beating and folding her batter, "for the crossroads of male and female, for the conflicts, for the intersection of lives, for the crossed swords and the shared chromosome! Ha. Or, A for the beginning, really, of all else. But since half of all marriages fail, a little a, a tentative a. Maybe M for maybe."

"Maybe C for *Che sarà sarà*," I smiled.

"Maybe W for Why on Earth," Ida groaned and then laughed. She turned her attention to the matzo box. "You have to modify. Marriages, like recipes, need modification." She tapped the box. "This recipe isn't half as nice as mine."

Hugh toddled into the kitchen quietly. He touched my knee and gave me a stern look and a heavy sigh. Inhaled. Exhaled. This meant he had exhausted the fun possibilities of Ida's house and it was time to go, but something about his demeanor worried me. I wondered if he had broken something out of sight and wanted to go, quickly now, before it was discovered. I tried not to bolt, but strolled with restraint to the living room. There, resting underneath the piano bench were: two dictionaries, one large plant, a handful of gravel carefully placed around the planter base, one stuffed monkey, one small bagel ort, some sheet music, a porcelain bird, and an embroidered pillow. He had made a crèche under the piano. Nothing was broken.

I returned to Ida's kitchen to find the peaceable Hugh freshly distracted on Ida's high stool. One cheek protruded and he seemed to be working on something large. He was overlooking her preparations for the matzo balls with mild boredom. But he watched with increasing interest as Ida plunged her hands into the batter, scooped out a scoop and began rolling it between her hands to make a ball.

"Hugh likes prunes," Ida said. "He is very good company. And I have lovely prunes. You, Hugh, are good company."

Hugh stopped chewing because of the authoritative tone in Ida's voice. Then she smiled at him, and I saw the jaws relax and return to his prune. My mother loved company in the kitchen.

Ida ripped a piece of wax paper and began setting her matzo balls on it in a grid. Spat! one went against the paper.

"I don't have time to put the batter in the refrigerator," she said. Spat! "Which makes it more difficult to roll the balls. But you can put the balls in the refrigerator afterward."

"Ida," I said, "all of this fuss about how different men and women are, all of this fighting about how we're not what the other is—does it matter in the end?"

"It matters until the asteroid hits," said Ida.

Spat!

"Fortunately for me," she added, "I shall probably be dead by that time. Sadly for you, and more so for your two darlings, the asteroid may be the earth's galactic exit. It may be uncomfortable, but it's marvelously cosmic."

Spat.

"In the meantime, it matters, yes, it matters that men and women are different because we have to share the planet somehow. I imagine the day will come when men will stop warring with one another and decide to war with women instead. What do you think of that?"

Spat.

Spat.

Spat.

"My first thought was that we would win," I said. "My second thought was that we would certainly lose."

Spat.

"Men are better fighters," Ida nodded. "They don't let anything intrude upon their warrior mission. In any event, it matters more for women than for men."

Spat.

"Women live their lives 'in relation to,'" she continued. "In relation to all around them. We are honeycombed by life, whereas men pass through more easily."

Spat.

I said, "Why don't we just shrug and try to get along, each female with her male, and stop pillorying the other for where they come up short? Why can't we just get on from here?"

"Ah yes," said Ida. "And why can't the Jews just put the Holocaust behind them?"

I saw myself skipping across a meadow when suddenly a great yawning abyss cracked open at my toes.

Spat!

"It's inhumanly rational," Ida said.

Spat!

Ida scooped the last bit of batter and slapped a last, littler matzo ball on the wax paper. Then she pushed the whole tray of soldiers to the side and pulled, with effort, a big steel pot from a cupboard in her kitchen island. On went the soup. Out came the chicken, carrots, onions, celery, stock, and spices. I watched her struggle to keep her hands steady. You needed your hands in the kitchen. They were your lieutenants. Ida was sometimes frustrated to the point of despair over the tremors of her fingers and her inability to command them better.

Ida gave one hand a curt shake. Be still, said her face, and she stared without blinking into the yellow of her old fingernails.

Ida's trembling came from age, but I wondered whether the sight of her own independently shaking hands made her think of Miriam, her poor plagued Miriam, now seventy-something and feeling slowly entombed.

"The Pope has Parkinson's, too," Ida said.

There was a sun porch off Ida's kitchen. The big door to it was divisible so that one could open the top half and leave the bottom closed like a gate. Miriam, when she was a little girl, made puppets and held puppet shows using the gate to make her stage. Sad, creative Miriam, painting the wall, making a stage of the kitchen's gated door, reminding Ida of her brilliance and pain several times each day. Miriam's melancholy would follow Ida to her grave. It would not chase her there, but it would be there at the end, when the ceiling blurred and the roar of an invisible wave rushed into Ida's translucent ears. Miriam's melancholy would stroke Ida's cheek.

Hugh, with half a prune still working his cheeks, banged on the gated door to go out onto the sun porch. He knew what awaited him there: Ida's two big stuffed animals, a trolley on wheels and on it a tray with a pitcher and six plastic cups, a croquet set, a planting bench filled with pebbles, furniture light enough to be skated across the slate floor, and a cordless telephone with blinking lights. There was no distracting Hugh with mere toys when a house with all its unassuming treasures waited upon his exploration. I zipped up his jacket and let him onto the porch where a small heating unit kept the winter at bay and a fragrant olive tree perfumed the air in channels. I passed through these channels, or pools, or superstrings, or however it was that scent materialized and moved itself, as I took a brief survey of breakables. Then I returned to the kitchen, where Madeleine was wearing a salad bowl on her head.

Ida pulled more eggs from the refrigerator. She was already thinking past her soup, to the linzertorte, which asked for eggs at room temperature. Maddie dropped carefully to the floor, from sitting to crawling position, to seize Ida's shoelaces, which flapped irresistibly. Ida looked down at her.

"When you can tie your own, darling, you can untie mine."

Ida pulled gently away and began her soup in earnest. It was not long ago, she once told me, that she had to pull the feathers from her chicken soup chickens. "I am old enough to remember," she would start her stories, "when the kitchen was as much a meat packing plant as a cooking hearth. In the country, the kitchen rightfully sat between the barn and the fire. You milked the cow in the barn, and you sieved the milk and boiled it in the kitchen hearth. Cooking food was secondary to cleaning your ingredients, at least a little, and making them palatable, sometimes. In the city, where I grew up, the Jews were always concerned with hygiene, and if you grew up in a Jewish Lithuanian-speaking ghetto in Boston, you boiled your t's before you crossed them."

After ninety-odd years, history sits up in the mezzanine of the mind, like an echo to current circumstances which have orchestra seats. I wondered in which decade, in which city, among which friends Ida was drifting as she salted and washed the chicken, scanned it for pin feathers, and dropped it, slush-plaff, into the stock. There was only plastic to remove these days, and salmonella to worry about, so women like Ida found themselves with a bounty of extra time in which they were no longer boiling diapers in the basement and plucking birds in the kitchen. Cooking had become more pleasurable, Ida told me, less arduous. She was always trying new recipes now, not flopping backward onto the soft couch of old ones. And if she didn't follow a recipe you gave her, she had the discretion not to tell you.

She threw a chicken neck-first into a pot of water and set it to cook while she turned to the vegetables. Count her carrots she did not. No ninety-three-year-old could seriously parse out carrots into a soup. Ridiculous. Ida chopped her carrots after scraping them indifferently over the sink. She used a large butcher's knife, but so carefully, a hand on the handle and a palm at the tip, slowly slicing down over the green caps of the carrot tops as though unconvinced her hands would do as bid, as if there had been rumors of their mutinous inclinations. She didn't cry as she cut up the onion, though God alone knew why not. And she scarcely washed the celery head before shivvying hunks of it into the pot. In went leeks, green and white, no roots. In went parsnips, snipped once at the belly. In went a shock of parsley, a spray of cloves, some bay leaves, a toss of ginger, a handful of black peppercorns, three taps of dried thyme from a jar.

You had to know how many chicken soups Ida had made over four score years to appreciate the way she handled this one, almost the way you had to know that Picasso could draw with photographic precision before you could truly appreciate his cubism; because what you saw first looked haphazard, flung into the soup pot, flung onto the canvas, untrained, immature. Couldn't an imbecile unwrap a chicken and bury it in water under a grocery bag of carrots, onions, and celery?

But it was the onlooker who needed training. The onlooker needed to be educated. Not every question really is a good question, and not every opinion has like merit. The mind needs honing to process well, and when unhoned minds make suppositions, they tend to be suppositions without value. Such an ugly truth to grace a morning.

So I gave Ida the benefit of the doubt, and I watched her, she who had made a kind of still life in her soup pot, with leaves and white bulbs and yellow chicken joints sticking out at odd angles. Each item was wedged in, beginning to swell, unfolding its cells and separating its flesh as the water warmed. Ida was humming, drawing into herself, preparing her soup in a pleasant solitude of sink and cutting board and burner. She was moving in small steps, back and forth from counter to island. And in her body you could see the years between birth and death, the closing of the circle, as a baby curls in with its shoulders, unfolds as it grows, and then, finally, curls inward again. The hunch of Ida's spine would not uncurl until the day she was laid out flat.

Ida worked at her soup as it sat in her pot. She approached it first with a paring knife, pruning and arranging it as a florist might arrange a vase of flowers, snipping here, reviewing there. Then she went at it with a long fork, digging like a gardener, unearthing things, culling. Her soup began to bubble and pop, and after ten minutes of tinkering with it, all the attendees sat cheek by jowl in the pot, under stock, upright, cooking. Her ingredients seemed like cheerful participants, as though they, too, had tickets to the seder.

Suddenly, she pulled back from the pot and smiled at it. Then she smiled at me. Then she smiled at Madeleine, who was eating Ida's pocketbook.

"This will be a very nice soup," Ida said to Madeleine. "And that, I hope, is a very tasty pocketbook."

And this is Ida's recipe for chicken soup:

# Ida's Chicken Soup for Matzo Balls

| | |
|---|---|
| 1 big chicken (5 to 6 pounds) with neck and giblets (not liver) | 2 small leeks, split and washed well |
| 12 cups water | 3 teaspoons kosher salt |
| 2 medium carrots | 1 handful black peppercorns |
| 3 celery stalks with leaves | 1 handful flat-leaf parsley |
| 1 medium onion | 1 teaspoon thyme |
| 2 parsnips | ½ teaspoon ginger |
| | 3 bay leaves |
| | Cloves and nutmeg |

Cover chicken with water and cook 2 to 3 hours, skimming foam. Midway, add vegetables and half the salt. Sieve soup and skim off fat. Pull chicken from bones, chop as desired and return to broth. Add some chopped vegetables and the spices. Salt to taste.

Company while you cook is desirable. Company to eat is critical.

I pulled Maddie from underneath the sink. The world was known to keep its household variety poisons under the kitchen sink. I set her by a drawer of towels and aprons, all folded into appetizing squares.

"Ida," I said, "have you heard about Ann's husband?" Ann was a mutual friend from the reading group.

Ida harrumphed softly. "He is a cad," she said. "And the new woman is a fool. But it is Ann who will lose. Ann and the children."

Ida and I had few friends in common. It limited our ability to chat about people and their ways without telling voluminous tales with introduction, plot, and summary. But I loved hearing her speak about men and women, because with Ida there was no such thing as gossip; there was ethical inquiry.

"He has served papers," I reported.

"That was fast."

There was a crash on the sun porch. Hugh had stumbled upon the fine effects of throwing Ida's heavy wooden croquet balls and mallets onto the bluestone floor. I ran out to deflect the game and proposed rolling them instead. We tried it together, but Hugh found little satisfaction in the act, the noise, or the result of rolling. So I moved the croquet set just off the sun porch and onto the back lawn. From the kitchen, we heard the dense thuds of croquet balls against cold earth. I watched through the gated door and beyond the windowed walls of the porch. Seeing this boy through two sets of glass made me reflect on my perceptions of his life, and I thought, yes, I am probably always looking through mild or immoderate distortions at him, although I love him, and he will always wish I had understood him better, that someone who loved him had been closer, not beyond the glass walls of gender or age or pure human separations. Such is the true aloneness of each soul, but Hugh, at least, was not now ruminating on his eternal solitude. He was thumping croquet balls, and his face lit up with each thump.

"Males like big thumps," said Ida. "All my girls enjoyed rolling those balls across the floor, finding secret routes and tunnels for them. My son, your son, all boys who have toured through this house have preferred great thumps and whacks."

"Ann's husband tells her he has fallen in love," I said. "True love."

"That is Ann's husband's great thump and whack," Ida replied. "And what happens when he tires of the game?"

"His feeling is that life is short and true love must be accommodated."

"My life has not been short."

"What if you're galloping through life and suddenly you come face to face with a truly great love? It stops you dead in your tracks. Should you not pursue it?"

Ida turned from her soup pot with concern. "What do you think?"

"If you have a family, I think you don't pursue it," I murmured. "I think protecting the family is crucial. Which is what I was hoping you would say, too."

"That is what I would say."

"But I know so many friends who would think I was crazy. They would think I was inhumanly rational."

Ida arched her brow. She looked suddenly very tired as she considered this conversation, the state of modern morality, and whether she had the energy to move into a linzertorte.

"Emotions must be recognized and bridled," Ida said. She began fishing for ingredients in the far recesses of her kitchen shelves. "If inhuman rationale is on one end of the spectrum, emotional slavery is on the other."

Klank went the sugar canister.

"It seems to me that modern marriages have more difficulty maintaining a happy medium."

Plunk went almonds from the freezer.

"Where is the rudder? It's too easy to list."

Clink went the brandy bottle onto the granite.

"Love, honor, duty to family, duty to self—these are all critical components in a marriage. It is not either love or honor, either duty to family or duty to self. People want it too simple nowadays. They want either-or so that it's easier to make their decisions. They want simple rules, so that they don't have to take responsibility for making a decision themselves."

Tac, tac, tac said three jars of wine-dark, blood-dark jam.

"I must sit a minute," Ida said, and we sat at her kitchen table quietly together. I set the hot water kettle to boil for tea and made a bottle for Maddie, who was eating a drawer. Three generations of women around a little round kitchen table all turned their eyes to the boy-child on the back lawn.

Hugh was standing in the middle of a spray of croquet pieces on the lawn. He had tired of his game. I watched him turn and spy the little goldfish pond to the left with its lily pads and frogs. An idea widened over his little face. He turned toward the house to see if we were watching, because it was clear to him that his wonderful idea had a risky sliver of grown-up reprobation attached. I guessed already: the croquet set, piece by piece, hurled into the little pond, preferably onto a frog first. He sidled in that direction. I was about to launch myself out there to intercept him, when Ida, who had also been enjoying the scene, said, "Ann always loved her husband for his boyishness. He is still a boy. What is it that brings a boy successfully into maturity, or doesn't?"

154

Ida always contrived to divert me from Hugh's activities. She would tell me that her house was childproof and I should bring both children, and then we would plunk down in her kitchen and shudder as we listened to Hugh explore more delicate rooms, or we would watch with fixed smiles as he disassembled her spice shelves, or we would forget to breathe as he made towers from her glasses within reach. This was what Ida loved, the brief incursions by known marauders on defined dates, and then their smiley departure, and peace. She needed boisterous youth to etch minute marks on her elderly hours.

So she raged on about the contemptible behavior of Ann's husband and distracted us from the back lawn, so that Hugh could be Hugh, outside, where the piano wasn't, where the china wasn't; where the cookie jar wasn't; and we sipped tea and didn't watch the croquet set fly and sink in the lily pond and wouldn't have heard a frog yelp if frogs yelped. Finally, Ida did happen to glance outside and suddenly released her speech. In this abrupt quiet, the wrapping of her words around my brain loosened and fell to the ground, and my eyes saw too clearly what was in front of them. Hugh, having failed to whop a frog with his croquet balls—all six of them—was now lowering himself carefully into the lily pond for the hand-to-hand portion of the battle.

"Oh dear," I murmured. "I'm sorry, Ida." I was thinking about the croquet balls and her beloved frogs and whatever else Hugh had thrown into those six inches of green water without my seeing.

"Your superego is too big," said Ida, laughing. "Bravo, Hugh!" she called out toward the pond.

My head flickered with images of twenty plump goldfish, belly-up, and a forensic expert saying, "It was a strong blow to the head . . ."

I had to laugh at myself.

"My father told me I looked too often in the rearview mirror," I said.

"That's a good way to describe it. An enlarged superego is nearly impossible to dampen, but the good part is that it keeps your standards high. Just don't push it onto your children if you can help it. That's the burden of being a woman: You can help yourself. Since you can, well then you must."

"And men?"

"Men can't help themselves. Not yet. Maybe by the time my great-grandchildren become adults, the male identity will be based on other than achievement, competition, and fantasy."

"Fantasy?"

"Fantasy. The fantasy of what defines masculinity. Imagine the repressive force of a little boy having to hide his erection. Penis envy!" Ida snorted. "What about men's womb envy?"

Man overboard. There were times with Ida when I couldn't follow her thought, when I missed the segues, and I would be left alone in the vast ocean of a pause, wondering whether I had fallen off the ship or whether there was no ship.

So often when I was a child, my mother would say to me, "Well, you know the Hegelian dilemma explained" such-and-such or so-and-so, and I didn't know, not ever, and I learned to hide well the fact that I'd lost the intellectual trail. It wasn't that I feared the revelation of my ignorance, but rather, I didn't want more information, I didn't want to learn more, I didn't want to be taught more, and especially not from my mother, no. I just wanted to be with her, wrapped in the sound of her voice, tied tightly into her company, so I learned to listen and not ask questions, and when I didn't understand the references to Braudel or Montaigne, I just let her words lap at my shores like waves until I could pick up a trace again in the sand. And here I was, some thirty years later in Ida's kitchen, listening and not asking questions. There were perhaps tiny lacunae, or gaps in uttering what the mind had grown tired of repeating? There were repetitions, because life was a litany of reiterating personal details within the circumference of friends and family. There were times when her train of thought jumped the tracks.

Ida stood up and began emptying bags of almonds into her blender.

"When I was sixty-five," she said, "my husband, the world-famous brain surgeon, said to me, 'Ida, you have taught me . . . how to be more social.'"

I looked hesitantly at Ida, and her face was frozen and fierce.

"So what!" she snapped. "How to be more social!" she hissed.

"There must have been so much he couldn't articulate," I murmured. I wished she could let it go, lose herself again in her linzertorte, but oh the pain of old wounds.

She said, "One day he came home from work and I had spent the day washing and scrubbing the house and four children, and he noticed a couple of toys left on the floor and said something critical about the children. So I said to him, 'Well, if you want your home run like an operating room, what are you going to do? Anesthetize them? Boil them in a pot to make them sterile?'"

Hurt sits in a cave. All the old hurts sit there together, so that if you walk into the cave you may confront many of them, all born on different days, and rage anew about the lot. I had rare glimpses into Ida's rage. The rage didn't disconcert me as much as the idea of being old and still feeling angry about something that had happened thirty-odd years ago, some eight-second snippet between husband and wife during the long journey of a marriage. She looked at me and said nothing. Her eyes were watery. My breath went short and sorrow pushed against my lungs. No one wanted to carry memories of hurt. My father had sometimes late at night decanted some fine old painful memory, keen and rich and perfuming his life still. His brimming eyes suggested that they had seen no intervening years, had never aged nor weakened, had preserved in their tears the perfect knowledge of his suffering.

Ida's thoughts drifted with her eyes slowly down to her cookbook.

"I need a cookbook for a linzertorte," she said. She looked down at Maddie, who was frowning up at her. "You will need a cookbook for a linzertorte, Madeleine. They are not intuitive cakes."

A broad smile cracked across Ida's face.

"If Beethoven had lived to be my age," she said, "he might've changed his tune, so to speak, and then where would I be? What kind of cake would I make? He might've gone soft, and then I could only make a sponge cake, no icing whatsoever. Now, if, say, Picasso inspired me to make a cake—and he wouldn't!—it would have to be a multiple-layer cake. It would be incredibly problematic, and not pretty. It would have frosting here and not there, and some of it would be one flavor and some of it another entirely. But Picasso was no cake's muse. He was a horrible man."

She tipped her head. "Although many women cook cakes for awful men."

I dragged Hugh inside the house kicking and screaming and wet. Hugh loved a good tantrum complete with flailing legs and blood-curdling protestations. The noise startled Maddie, who had most of her little body inside an open cupboard. She pulled back to look. Her eyes widened with alarm but she said nothing. Maddie was an observer. I would see her taking in her brother's daily behavior and calculating what she would like to do herself one day. She was very purposeful. She worked steadily and without noise at her self-appointed missions: rolling over, standing, bending, reaching, eating with a spoon. She wasn't taking her own development lightly. I suspected if I looked at the inside rail of her crib, I would find check marks etched. Did it. Did it. Did it.

Ida was delighted to find Maddie occupying the space that the big soup pot left vacant. She bent down to steady a tiny elbow. Ninety-three years stooped to steady twelve months. I heard her telling Maddie how easy soups were, too easy, in fact, for educated women "like the two of us" to dawdle with.

"With soups, you have to train your thoughts to be active elsewhere," Ida instructed.

Clang clang went a set of pot lids.

I brought Hugh into the living room to reinterest him in interior possibilities. I threw a sofa blanket over the piano bench crèche and he disappeared into this fort save for one wet, booted foot that tapped against the carpet. I loved that about Hugh, the way he would say I AM GONE with ninety percent of his body, the last ten percent be damned. It was his wonderful certainty, his unwavering belief in the story he had created. Hugh was amusing himself with invisible bandits, befriending them by singing the alphabet, by telling them his numbers up to twenty.

I tiptoed back to the kitchen. At the doorway I heard Ida saying to Maddie, "If Beethoven had lived to be ninety-three, he would have tried to hang around to meet me."

Maddie wriggled her feet in agreement.

"Temptress!" Ida grinned at her. She paused to study her ingredients.

Ida once told me that at her age, she wanted more than ever to cook well—the product of so many years of considered practice.

"This is not chicken soup," she said to Maddie, who was watching her like a patient falcon. "You have to think. You have to assess the measurements. Otherwise, you might find yourself racing to the supermarket in *medias res*."

Ida ground her almonds until she had just over two cups. Then she peered down at the baby again and said, "It's good to be a temptress now and then."

"Ida," I said, "what if it were me having the affair with Ann's husband?"

"Then you would be a fool." Ida turned a cold face from her recipe. "Margaret Mead thought people should have three marriages in life: The first for passion, the second for parenting, the third for companionship."

"And?"

"And she destroyed her children. She was brilliant and hopelessly selfish. Ann's husband is not brilliant but equally selfish. You—if it is you—are acting the fool, and a dangerous fool. You would be inflicting anguish on several lives, and don't think you wouldn't be responsible, even in the name of your ridiculous true love."

"But how can true love be ridiculous?"

"That is the question of a child."

"Could you forgive me if I told you it were me?"

Ida paused. "Oh yes, over the years. But you would never know it because I'd be dead by then."

We were both quiet. I had pressed in soft spots. Maddie was watching me intently.

"It's not me," I said, to Maddie mostly.

"I'm glad," Ida replied.

It was August in the year 1904, sultry and oppressive, when Ida's mother, Mamie, twenty years old and just off the boat from Lithuania to Boston, carried her baby through the hot, breezeless summer of an immigrant ghetto. It was her first child. A baby girl born to a girl. Ida Alice, growing plump and wriggling through the torpor of the ninth month. Ida had a photo of her mother in the locket around her neck, a locket given to her by a young woman whose own mother once tried to keep Ida from buying land in town. Ida was by then the wife of a famous brain surgeon, but no amount of fame would smooth the transition of Jews into that neighborhood. Years later Ida helped the daughter through a messy adolescence, then a horrible divorce, and finally the trials of single motherhood. She wore the locket around her neck with love and irony. On the face was a porcelain painting of flowers rimmed by tiny pearls. Ida had it slung onto something like rope, but I never asked why. Why no pretty chain? Maybe the rope was a memory of the young woman's mother and the nooses she tried to tie around so many necks, including her daughter's.

Inside the locket were small oval pictures of Mamie at twenty-two, and Ida at four, both faces round and sturdy and staring outward with the kind of near ferocity that is solemnity, dignity, and pride. Look at me, commanded the photographer, and hold still, still, still, until the sitter falls into a calcified glower for the camera. I never saw a picture of Ida's father.

"So," Ida said, working the linzertorte dough with her fingers, "did I tell you I had a heart attack?"

"Another?"

"No. Just one. So I told you."

Rats. Ida loved to tell these stories. Rats, said her face now, because that opportunity had come and gone.

"I need to call you once a week," I chirped, "because it seems whenever I don't call, you go and hurt yourself, or fall down and have a heart attack."

"You're mixing me up with your mother," Ida said.

Oh, I groaned inwardly. When friends are therapists by training! I had told Ida about my mother over the years, although I had no distinct memory of which stories. I must have recorded the homecomings, after days or weeks of not seeing my mother, when I would find her so altered, so disfigured by cancer. Had I told her about the last horrible fall? Wasn't I joking to Ida about having to call more often to prevent her accidents? Was it possible for me to joke or was my unconscious always revising and spewing out jokes that were not funny?

"I was kidding," I said to Ida.

"Harrumph." She was not.

I flushed with anger. I was no open-faced sandwich, I wanted to say. But I didn't know whether it was true or not. I sighed noisily.

Ida broke her dough into roughly two-thirds, one-third lumps. The larger lump she lay in a tart pan, gently pressed it across the bottom and nudged it up the sides.

She said, "Do you know, I had this kitchen totally remodeled when I was eighty-eight. When most people my age were winding down, calling it quits, I was starting over."

Not wholly. She put in new cabinetry—quiet cupboard doors— and granite countertops. She installed drawers that didn't need tugging, a state-of-the-art refrigerator, new ovens, an island, discreet lighting. She bought new cookware, colanders, and machinery, and then she abandoned the machinery for hand-chopping and hand-kneading. The bread machines and fancy blenders sat at one end of a counter, in a dark corner, like expensive tractors once left on the wooded shores of Mozambique to rust and rot because somebody in the West thought fine machinery belonged everywhere, but they didn't belong there, in the jungle, not then.

What Ida didn't replace were the old cookbooks, gravy-spattered, scribbled with revisions. From such a one came the linzertorte recipe. I sat watching her spread purple-black jam, bruise-black jam, across the bed of blond dough, and this is the recipe she swore she was using that morning, although I saw her put in more ground almonds than asked for, and goodness knows what else she got up to while we talked.

# *Ida's Linzertorte*

1 cup unsalted butter
1 cup sugar
3 eggs, separated
1 tablespoon brandy
1 lemon, grated rind
   and juice

½ pound almonds,
   finely chopped
2 cups flour, sifted 3
   times with 1
   teaspoon baking
   powder
Jam or preserves

Cream butter and sugar well. Add yolks, brandy, lemon peel, and juice, then almonds and flour, sifted and mixed with baking powder, lastly beaten whites. Roll or pat two thirds of dough and line a springform with it, bottom thicker than sides. Fill with fine jam. Roll remaining dough, cut into strips, and place crisscross on top. Bake at 350°. Before serving, fill any holes on top with jam. Freezes well.

It was time for us to go. Ida was exhausted from standing and needed to be alone. The cooking was nearly done. The children were itchy. Only it was so hard to go, each time. What if I were never to see her again, what if I were saying good-bye for good and had to put Ida in that inside/outside place where my mother, my daughter, and Don were? What if Ida were never to call again and tell me she had been baking bread into the small dark hours of the night?

"Are you tired?" I once asked her. "Have you had enough?"

"I can't go yet," she teased. "Too many people need me. Too many patients."

"So, you're not tired."

"My body is tired," Ida conceded. "I've spent almost a year mourning the loss of my abilities. But loss leads to change, and you have to make the change positive. Loss can lead to liberation. You have to use the energy you spend mourning in some more productive way. You have to transcend the disintegrations of your body. Otherwise, you're just a cemetery of capabilities lost. You have to remake your image of being elderly. Anyone can do it. I am Exhibit A."

As she gently rolled the last piece of linzertorte dough into a thin sheet and cut strips to lay across the top, she said, "Did I tell you I saw an interesting couple yesterday? They're new patients. He treats her like a doormat and she has tired of it. Hooray!" Ida paused. "Of course she doesn't feel too happy with the change. She's unaccustomed to self-worth."

"Does a marriage last when the woman suddenly tires of the status quo?" I asked.

"Not often, not in cases like this. Usually there's a divorce, and the man goes out and remarries someone else he can treat like a doormat. There are plenty of women out there who would love to be treated like doormats. The woman who decides those days are over has to reinvent herself. It's not easy. And there were some nice things to being a good doormat. It was nice cleaning off the soles of shoes *well*. By the way, I have an extra jar of this nice jam from the Simmons College Alumnae Group. I only used two in the torte. Do you suppose your little marvels would enjoy it on toast?"

165

Ida was already tucking the jar into my diaper bag. I went off to tidy up her living room, to corral and bejacket my children, and when I returned, she was fixing the top of the linzertorte, adjusting the lattice, adding bits of jam so that it would be beautiful, a Beethoven symphony in almond and raspberry.

"She was a very nurturing wife," Ida said.

"The doormat?"

"Yes. And very accomplished, too. A pianist. Mother of four children by him. None of them are in jail. But all of them, one after another—sometimes all of them at once—draw from her well, and they don't replenish the water supply." Ida turned to me. "So, who nurtures the nurturer?"

She didn't expect an answer. Ida loved rhetorical flourishes. Then she said, "Who nurtured your mother?"

"I don't know," I sighed. "It's the part I missed, the part where I could ask her things like that."

"You could also say she escaped," Ida grinned mischievously. She slipped the linzertorte into the oven and set the timer. "Escaped your examination."

"*There's* irony. Because my mother didn't escape much in her short life."

"I have some homework for you," Ida said at the door. "Tell me three things your mother did that you didn't like, and don't repeat them. Then tell me three things your mother did that you did like, and see if you can repeat them for Hugh and Madeleine."

"I like that she was in the kitchen," I blurted.

Ida smiled. Her chicken soup simmered below a chimney stack of steam on the stove top.

"The kitchen is the laboratory of life," she said.

# 6

## *Too Many in the Kitchen*

I FILL THE SINK with water and swirl in fresh sandy lettuce
leaves. Red oak, bibb, endive, romaine, radicchio. The lamb's
tongue will be the last to give up the garden soil at the bunching
of its stems. Circling red and green and white in the basin, this
melee of leaves reminds me that life is full of orbiting bodies,
most with no organizing sun, no center, no "around which." After
my mother died, I realized that she had been the center of my
orbit. It took me years to find a center in myself so that I might
join the human swirl.

Hugh calls me. He *needs* a glass of juice. Stop everything. Finally it was my turn to become the center of another creature's
orbit, as a mother. In that organic way, in the slow and robotic
unfolding that plants do, we move into childbearing age, yearn
for children, have them, yearn for a return to ourselves, have it,

die. It seems like a built-in code, a conspiracy of proteins that pushes us forward as adults, just as it did when we were infants, as we wriggled, crawled, toddled, walked, ran, wrought havoc on a house that became ours. We all want to create our parenthood differently, and better, and then we are humbled by the unadjustable demands of children, the sleeplessness, the vulnerability. The similarity of experience among parents is startling. Sometimes motherhood seems as mindless as a game of leapfrog, in which you clear your hurdles and then you are a hurdle to be cleared.

I pull out a colander to dry the lettuce. Maddie has spotted Hugh's cup. She *needs* juice, too. Stop everything.

Nothing more than interruption characterizes the first years of motherhood. A mother becomes the local train, stopping at every station and arriving last at every endpoint. In the beginning, it's lovely to be so needed, but the evolution of feelings doesn't stop there. Gradually the desire grows to mail a letter and spread the peanut butter without detailed explanations or assistance. I practice saying "Out of the kitchen!" with a smile, the cheery intonations masking my rigid spine. But my children are outraged. There is foot-stamping, defiant glares. My children aren't afraid of me. Moreover, they see our kitchen as belonging to them, not me. It's our little Battle of the Bulge.

I probe the basket of lettuce leaves once more. Our vegetable garden sits under a tree with dripping needles. The lettuces collect them.

Hugh is back. Hugh *needs* a marble. I'm tempted to tell him to look under the refrigerator, but the humor would be lost on him, and frankly, it's scary under there. I pull two marbles from a drawer, thinking "how clever am I" to satisfy Maddie's next need before she knows it.

"One for each of you," I say.

In a small bowl, I whisk vinegar and oil together, add a teaspoon of strong mustard and one of sugar. Some pontificating bullfrog once told me vinaigrettes were hopeless without a chopped shallot. Three hundred and sixty-three days of the year, I have no shallots. *Ribbit.* But I never force anyone to eat my salads.

My kitchen became a different universe once I had children, not because they wound themselves around my ankles or hung on my apron strings or mined the floors with toys; and not because I lost the use of several cabinets and with them the stashes of canned goods and sacks of flour and sugar that I hadn't realized made such interesting percussions and unlikely towers and powdery cumulus clouds; and not because the kitchen inflated overnight with foreign foods such as formula and cereal and purees that I couldn't possibly think of tasting myself but that I nonetheless spooned down willing throats; the kitchen became a different place because it was suddenly so sticky.

My kitchen became something eerie, like a room in a spooky story where first your hands stick to the knobs, then your bottom sticks to the chair, your skirt is laminated to the counter, and you can't move at all because you're glued to the floor. People say, "I love what you've done to your cupboards!" and you gasp, because you hadn't seen it—the yogurt, the finger paint, the carrots in the hinges. Fortunately, for me a kind of Jackson Pollock design of apple juice strewn across the hardwood floor in loops and swags is heaven, not only because I could never afford a real Jackson

Pollock, not only because I prefer the results of my children's Process to those of his Process, but because the loss of our first baby made me yearn for any sign of healthy child-life.

Maddie taps my thigh with a book.

"Not now," I say gently.

She waits, as though I have said nothing at all.

I dry my hands and lift her up onto the counter. She loves to flip the pages up here where toast is sprinkled with cinnamon and berries are folded into batter. Her company is my essential ingredient, no matter the recipe. It's practical for me as well, because my feet are cemented to the floor with the morning's orange juice.

Maddie's book has illustrations of little creatures standing on the crests of convex lines, and that is the world, and we stand *on* it, *on top* of it. It's a steadying thought to be on top of a world that is known to be spinning around the sun at 66,600 miles per hour; indeed, it is a wonder I don't have to hold on to the edge of the kitchen countertop, reach out an arm to stop the flour and sugar canisters from sliding over the edge as we whip around. What wonderful comedy that every creature on earth envisions itself as standing firmly on top of that convex line. We have to think we're on top to survive, because no one could live with the image of being a horizontal object or even an object tipped head-downward into black space, flung into a web of gravity by the inconceivably rapid revolutions of the immense and still partially molten rock we call Earth.

Dizzy with imagery, I set Maddie down on terra firma.

"We are our own North Pole," I say to her, too young to be injured by her mother's predatory scientologies. To be fair, I once contradicted Hugh when he told her that the snow was eating her red rubber ball, left out on the frozen lawn and slowly disappearing under the lumpy white. Sometimes I feel obliged not to let all the lies dance, but to make wallflowers of a few of them, and to lend a hand to the nearsighted schoolteacher, in the next millennium, who will try to teach my children elementary science.

Maddie wasn't listening to me anyway when I told her about the true magnetic north. She had broken into a box of tea and, perhaps irritated by the gauzy bags, was beating them with a wooden spoon. But I heard myself, amused myself, and provoked myself to wonder, well, if this were one pole, what would be the other? Rather, if the kitchen were one pole in a woman's world, what would be at the other end? What is the opposite of Kitchen? The War Room? The bedroom?

I empty the sink of spiders and pine needles and water made green by the lettuce. The last thing you think will stain is lettuce.

"Maddie," I say, "a woman's life is punctuated only by semicolons, until she comes to the period at the end. She has no North Pole, she has no linear construct, she has only momentum and her connection to the past through a mother and her connection to the future through a daughter."

This was somewhat disturbing. I had arrived at the image by linking phrases, as I linked my children's engines and box cars; but without my mother, my own link to the past was fractured. My link to the future was pulling rubber bands from a drawer.

I step between spirals of spilled juice to draw a salad bowl from a cupboard. *Pock!* goes somebody's cup on the floor. I stop everything.

My children don't interrupt me while I clean the floor. They seem to feel included while they watch. Funny how they don't feel implicated.

I return to the sink. There is a basket of greens that must belong to someone. There is a children's book open on the countertop, as though it had a recipe to offer. There is a rejected rubber band. I have a sense that I've just woken up in a foreign train station and am given over to a pleasurable review of its architecture before I have to deal with being lost. My kitchen belongs on a Dali canvas.

"Jelly toast, jelly toast," chant two hungry children, prancing on their toes.

While they are small, I belong to them. Their lives are like streams of needs. One day they will walk out my kitchen door, the familial launch pad, and I will only be able to watch. May they fly. All those preparatory years of words—encouragement and caution—will dissolve like sky-writing into the vast blue of their private heavens.

I pull out a volume of Greek myths to read to the children while they eat and flip to the story of Icarus. But a wrinkle forms across my brow.

"Mama has no dinner for Daddy," I say, with a vague memory of a salad. The children stop chewing. They expect me to pass through troubled moments the way they do. I am offered a piece of jelly toast.

"Happy Mama," explains Hugh. "No sad. No mad. No worried." (Pronounced *wuwwied*). "Just happy."

We decided to make the kitchen a little bigger to accommodate our enlarged family. Every year I noticed my pots growing in size, glasses growing in number, accidents growing in proportion. I thought expansion was a reasonable idea, but as the project materialized, I grew gloomy. Questions were coming my way like machine-gun fire, and I, the pacifist, said, "Bright. Sunny. Bigger. I don't care about the rest of it."

Whoa! said the architect.

Whoa! said the general contractor.

Whoa! said my husband.

So I educated myself a bit about kitchens. I went to the appliance store, I begged the oil and gas company to give me a propane tank, I learned to pronounce the name of a dishwasher that was small and quiet and made in a country whose alphabet is different. The architect commended me on matching the countertop color with the flooring. The cupboards are painted Opalescence, the trim is Navajo White, the counters Dune Pink. Pleasing and transporting images. But that's where the poetry stops in my kitchen, like the abrupt edge of a desert; from there on, it's only the gritty sticky truth.

After the choices were made on paper, I could have left the community for a month. Nothing arrived on time, and much of what arrived was a mistake. The contractor got irritable, fast. Everybody started leafing through the contracts for clauses about liability, and I had no kitchen and hence, no home. You think living in the suburbs is relatively tranquil, in fact crushingly dull, until you do some house remodeling and suddenly what few men remain in the vicinity by day come crashing down on your front door with faces that say, "I'd work in the city if I could, too, because hell is answering to women for kitchen remodeling."

Overall I like our house, an old Victorian farmhouse with spa-

cious rooms, tall ceilings, and a cheerful spirit. The kitchen required alligator-wrestling, though, and there are some issues that
will forever bubble to the surface of the swamp waters. For instance, there is no table in my kitchen. I believe kitchens need
tables, and so there are always a few trying to get in, creeping up
to the doorways, edging the corners of their useful tabletops into
view. One would almost have thought my kitchen was being be-
sieged by tables and holding its fort against the marauders.

"I don't think we'll be able to open the refrigerator door," said
my husband, looking thoughtful and nervous as I lugged an old
porcelain-top table into the center of the kitchen.

Who are you? I felt like saying. This is my space.

But, "We need a kitchen table," I said simply.

My husband was bewildered.

"There," he pointed. He pointed ten feet away to a window
with a big old table.

I squinted in that direction.

It's actually in the same room, as is the children's play area.
We made a big L-shaped room that people admire. Other people.
Kitchen on one leg, eating area in the corner, children's room on
the other leg.

"You need a table *in* the kitchen," I said.

"But why?" he asked.

"So that my friends can cry here."

Because that's where we all go, I thought to explain, to find
comfort. Our foreheads sink onto our forearms as though the
weight of the world's gender discrepancies were slumped on our
shoulders. There at our kitchen tables so much is aired, resolved,

left behind. If the bedroom defines the contours of a marriage, the kitchen table is where the contours of a family are reckoned.

I was heard. My husband's eyes read "alien" but he tramped around the kitchen with a measuring tape and a sketch pad. He showed me the pure scientific impossibility of any furniture fitting in there, as though it would soothe me. "I'm afraid you're going to have to cry over here," he said, and pointed outside the box of his charming blueprint.

"You should draw more," I said, always distractable, but undeterred. I took his pad and sketched in a table with a mug and a wailing figure, and it felt the way it looked—a figure in empty space, sobbing about being a figure in empty space.

"A kitchen table is an anchor," I said as I drew. "Without it, I drift."

I gave the drawing to my children and they colored it yellow and purple and red. We were their anchors; for them the kitchen table could be yellow and purple and red and in the attic, and it was all right.

# 7

## *Laura*

YOU SHOULDN'T LEAVE a woman alone in the kitchen too long. Things happen. She begins to hum Edith Piaf songs. Her women friends come over for strong coffee and stronger cheese. For a while they talk about schools for their children, presidential politics, the demoralization of our culture, good swingsets; then, with the first taste of bread and cheese together, there is some silent sharing of pleasure in the compatibility of the pale colors— bread the color of a Jersey cow, cheese a sheep's-wool white— and the mixing of textures, one porous and gently resistant, the other opaque and melting. Finally, after a pause, the conversation surges into the delta of mankind and womankind, creeps first into the larger waterways of habit, flows slowly between the trees of marriage, nudges softly but persistently against the small islands of children, and gradually fills in over the topography of daily history, flooding the whole land at last until it takes the form of a lake, still and broad, although it is really a delta, fingerlike, branching, a place in between river and sea.

It demands a lifetime, this conversation of women about men, because the connections and abrasions between them are so vast, wide, beautiful, unknown, concealing, murky, procreative, strangling, forever refreshed, and forever bogged down. The talk of women is like the hum of a distant universe that men know exists, although they can't see it, and it surrounds them, becomes part of the white noise, or blue noise, or red noise, depending upon the threat it poses or the pleasure it accords. We bend over our coffees, letting the soft steam warm our cheeks, and talk about the way women stack up into a column of shared experiences, and men orbit in a million different trajectories.

When I am in my kitchen, life seems to run like rapids between the banks of my countertops, and I feel like a pylon in the stream, sunk for a pier that will never be built. Here is my mind's life. The shared words of women friends drench me and the stretching limbs of children bed themselves like oysters all around me. I tie on an apron, remove myself from the world outside, and I lay myself bare to the world inside.

My mother knew early on that a woman has to invent her married life on her own, because her husband will never understand her needs, the breadth of her capacity and loneliness; and she was therefore able to love my father with continuity, with the kind of maternal compassion that we all feel for our boy children and are shocked to have to summon for our husbands. They are not the same creatures as us, and for us to keep pounding upon their sensibilities and suspect that a little more anger, a few more threats, a larger description, a lawyer, might move them to understand us . . . well, then we are the pathological desperados.

My friend, Laura, is less forgiving of the gap between male and female, and finds gender differences an excuse for abandoning the woman to the kitchen and children.

"I'm angry," she said to me once while we stood in her little slot of a kitchen. She abandoned her declaration there, open as the Pacific Ocean, unpegged to one event, large and flat, as though we might all be drifting across one uninterrupted response to life—mine sadness, hers anger, another's revenge.

"Nothing much matters before children," she said. "Before motherhood there is a larky delusion of equality that haunts marriages."

I watched her make dinner as she spoke. She had found a recipe in the newspaper that appealed, an Asian stir-fry for which she had to buy lemongrass, which was now lying in a bundle to the side, threateningly.

"Which part do you use?" Laura asked me, prodding the lemongrass with her knife tip, threateningly back. It seemed abducted there, bound and gagged with rubber bands. Like a leek, it was a vegetable with a bottom and a top, but leeks came with roots to show you up from down, and Laura's lemongrass gave no such clue. It was enigmatic.

"Very yin and yang," I said.

She looked up at me round-eyed. She wasn't looking for humor. There was no yin and yang in that apartment, there was no half-this-half-that, no harmony so pure it made you sleepy. There was Edge in those five rooms, and Edge forced all things to quick and clear declaration. Lemongrass was to declare its edible end. Children were to declare their needs. Edge didn't tolerate whining children, wishy-washy dialogues, or inscrutable vegetables.

"You're brave to try this recipe," I said, glancing down at the scrap of newsprint that was blotting onion juice in silence, supping up the fluids on the countertop like a burglar. "Do you like to cook new things?"

"No," Laura said, and she sliced into the lemongrass to see what information a cross-section would offer, her face a study of impatience and begrudging interest.

Laura did cook new things, regularly, pushing like Sisyphus against the downward momentum of a husband, her second, who said nothing appreciative at the table.

"No more surprise salads," he said once, heaving more than gravity against her improvisations.

"Did you blanch the red pepper?" he'd say, sarcastically, rhetorically, into the silence of a first bite.

It was enough to stifle most inspirations in advance, but not Laura's, which were born not in the love of foodstuffs and marvelous flavors, but in the knowledge that life was full of doing things you didn't want to do. The comments hurt, regularly, and became the subject of phone calls. It was a small slight to be unappreciated for earnest endeavor; to be reproved was a mean thing, like nicking the head off a flower.

"I don't pretend to cook the ten-thousand-franc dinner at the Café Anglais," Laura said, deflated, calling one evening after a wild rice salad had been wilted with a phrase. "I don't need a ballet review."

"Stop cooking his dinner," I suggested. "If he doesn't appreciate your cooking, which is the result of planning, shopping, and preparation, don't do it. Break the pattern."

But good support and bad advice sometimes go hand-in-hand, because love is not practical. Laura was reluctant to raze the dinner bridge, so she built a detour by cooking plain rice and plain pasta and leaving the sauces to him. She had to work it out, alone, tailored to her own marriage; because marriages are mysteries and kitchens are workshops of alchemy and women must connect their dreams with family realities right there at the pasta pot.

Meanwhile Laura cooked for the children, who liked her meals. They would tell me about the tortellini with spinach, or the corn salad. They wanted it again.

"I need to get a recipe from you," I said, remembering a dish she had made that even she enjoyed.

Laura laughed. "A recipe? From me? But I don't cook."

But she did cook, because she had to.

"My mother wrote," I recalled, "that if you didn't have children, you could nonconform all the hours of the day, but if you were a mother, you had to play house."

"Absolutely," said Laura. "And it would be so much more fun if you were just pretending to play house." She chuckled. She, who carted a family's laundry up and down the elevator; she, who lugged the family's groceries from parking lot to elevator to apartment; she, who stood for hours in the kitchen, a telephone in the crook of her neck, trying to hear past the commuter trains rattling back and forth four stories down. There—with as much counter space as a child's desk, the staples crammed and stacked on top of the pots and mixing bowls behind dark-stained cupboard doors, the children's artwork and baseball schedules and a list of pious reminders on how to deal with children when they're about to make you a murderess, all this paper flapping thick against the refrigerator under the law of industrial magnets—there was Laura, playing house.

Her role was about to enlarge. There was to be a stage change. They had bought a house and would be moving soon.

"You will have timothy grass, crabgrass, and onion grass," I said. "And no more lemongrass."

Soon Laura would have an ample kitchen with a table and chairs. I would miss this closet, in which we inhaled to pass one another. I had grown accustomed to standing there with her, our hips leaning in Renaissance S-curves against the lower cupboards, our arms engaged in food and thought like Perugino angels in Elysium, though we were hardly weightless, but rather leaden on linoleum, awkward creatures batting our opacity against the opacity of stove and countertop in a graceless Virginia reel of making meals for our families.

The drawings for Laura's new kitchen included a flow chart that looked like the choreography for a tidier dance. There was a triangle drawn between the refrigerator, the stove, and the sink. A pencil line linked it to an island countertop. Food Preparation Station, it said.

"Where do I stand?" I asked.

"Sit. You sit there," Laura pointed.

"While you cook . . . there."

Laura laughed. "I told you. I don't cook."

She handed me a damp swatch of newsprint. It was the recipe for her Asian stir-fry. "Keep it," she said. "You cook."

So here is Laura's recipe, and her children liked it, and my team liked it, and I don't remember what her husband said but I'm sure it wouldn't enhance the meal.

## Laura's Asian Dinner

3 tablespoons peanut oil
1 cup coconut milk
¾ pound boneless
chicken sliced into
thin strips
2 cloves garlic finely
minced
1 stalk lemongrass finely
chopped
½ cup minced scallions

Zest of one lemon
2 tablespoons chunky
peanut butter
2 teaspoons
coriander
1 tablespoon sugar
(optional)
Salt and pepper to
taste

Heat oil in skillet until very hot. Add chicken, garlic, lemongrass and scallions. Toss frequently. Add ⅓ cup coconut milk. Lower heat to moderate. Add peanut butter, coriander, sugar, and salt and pepper to taste. Let cook five minutes. Stir in lemon zest and ⅓ cup coconut milk, more if desired for consistency, and let simmer for five minutes or until the chicken is cooked through. Serve with jasmine rice.

*Laura's notes:* You use the purple part of the lemongrass; plain white rice is fine. It wasn't bad but it wasn't the Taj Mahal.

⁓

"Do you know what?" Laura pinned me against the refrigerator one day. *Conclusion* had pasted her round eyes wide open. "I am not a kind person."

Uh-oh.

"You're awfully nice to me," I murmured. "Your phone is ringing."

She reached for the phone but spun on me once more. "Nice is not the same thing as kind."

This had the makings of a Grand Inquisition, in which I would be coerced to tell my interrogator she was a cur. Laura hung up.

"Nice is behavior," she continued. "Kind is disposition." She set two and one quarter cups of salted water to boil.

"So when you are nice to me, you're surmounting your heartless nature," I said. "Your phone is ringing."

I took the opportunity to review her box of rice. Women have an endless hunger for chatting up brands of food, as though they might learn something earth-shivering that would affect their loyalty to a certain rice; as though brands of supermarket food testified to moral choices—something characterizing the mettle of another household.

When Laura hung up, she gave me a big shrug. "I am not a kind person," she insisted. She poured a heaping cupful of rice into the boiling water. "I just try hard to overcome it."

"You raise children. You work. You keep house. You quash your baser basic instincts. That's a full day. Why do you buy this rice?"

The phone rang.

The defining aspect of Laura's closet kitchen was the telephone. It hung by the doorway, insinuating that the space, minus cutlery and oven, would have made a better phone booth. From it dangled a spiral cord so long that I imagined she could be down the block at the playground and still connected in conversation. Laura prepared meals with the phone tucked into her neck. That was her company in a kitchen without chairs. There were the voices and the stories while she chopped, stirred, poured, doled out. She could sip a glass of wine and slip garlic slivers into a lamb while the narrations of a friend spilled into her ear. She set the table while discussing issues of work, marriage, weekends. She polled for juice options while murmuring support to friends in a quandary. She had no chair in that kitchen, but she had this telephone, and each time it rang there was, for Laura, a smiling face at the back door.

Laura didn't want to be left alone in the kitchen, although she preferred it to having children underfoot. Chopping basil was not a mantra. Doing only one thing at a time bothered her, as it bothers most women, as if they were properly an apartment building with productive residents on all floors at all times. You see such women, darning needles protruding from their mouths as though they had bitten a porcupine, their hands working a piece of cloth while they rocked a cradle with one foot and listened to Mozart or Blondie on the stereo. In the kitchen they will have a pie, a salad, and a fricassee going at once, carefully not tipping the mountain of chopped green onions into the pie, not putting the tablespoon of tapioca into the fricassee. They will hold pencils in their mouths the way flamenco dancers hold their roses, because the telephone rang twenty minutes ago with a friend with a number, and the pencil was without a tag that said "Drop me," because this was not the White Rabbit's hole.

Women tend to worry that they're wasting time. I worry about it a lot, as I let my index finger drag in the spigot's stream waiting for warm water to emerge from the kitchen pipes. Not that making bottles for infants is a waste of time. Not that the care and feeding of the animal commonly referred to as the Family is a waste of time. Not that retrieving marbles from underneath the refrigerator is a waste of time. Maybe the ferrying of those offspring to baseball diamonds meets the test of tedium, but then, who else the ferryman? Maybe the careful folding of all those undershirts into drawers where little hands rummage mercilessly could appear silly at first glance, until you wait thirty years for the chrysalis to crack open and your child flutters into adult life and is happier for the stowed experience of his baby cottons carefully folded and tucked away.

In fact, women flunk free time and gaze longingly upon their partners who seem so content to be motionless in front of televisions in spite of, or perhaps because of, a child's wails haunting the background. Women are forever jumping up from their chairs as though some nervous condition rendered them painfully committed to the upkeep of the world at large, as though folding towels was at least a small step toward atoning for man's injustices to mankind. Women cannot slow themselves down, whether it be in their determined self-destruction, their determined self-preservation, or their determined self-improvement. I see it in Laura. There is something of the missile in her, something launched and powerful.

"You know who else wasn't kind?" Laura asked me.

"Medea," I offered. "Now there's a problem in controlling your instincts."

"Vita Sackville-West," Laura said, filling in the blank correctly. The phone rang.

Laura had been reading about the Bloomsbury group, and her book sat on the counter under two cucumbers. Laura read while standing at the school bus stop. She read while rice cooked. She read late into the night. I never knew someone who stole moments like Laura, despairing because her life had been made to fit a larger frame—twenty-six-hour days and thirteen-month years—and she was condemned forever to cropping her existence and pilfering minutes.

Laura would have enjoyed life in the circle of Virginia Woolf and Vita Sackville-West, "taking dinner" instead of making it, marveling over a hunk of bread and butter outdoors because she has not cut and spread it herself six times daily indoors. Laura has tried to live a life of ideas that excludes the wash, the stowing of fresh milk, the sharing of recipes. She has reached longingly toward the man's life, as though his were more validly a life of the mind, as though the joy and slogging through of child-rearing were less stimulating, less productive, less enriching; and so, the cooking and dressing and washing slap up against her bow over and over, in their mundanity. She persists in veering the conversation away from what her hands are doing, vigorously insisting that it interests her not one bit, and betraying stalks of real pain, the way little flowers distract you from the large weed they're on.

"Would you have wanted to be the kind of mother she was?" I asked, referring to Sackville-West's loose connection with the raising of her children.

"Did the children turn out all right?" Laura asked back.

I shrugged noncommittally. "Wrote a fairly damning biography of her," I muttered, thinking that would be the worst of all possible fates.

Laura arched her brows.

"I can just imagine a cookbook from Virginia Woolf and Vita Sackville-West," I said. "Word salad, wit stew. How clever we would be wasting away from malnourishment."

Laura pushed her book off the counter and set to peeling cucumbers. "There was a woman in their circle who went to Egypt and alphabetized it. That was the only way she could deal with it."

"You could alphabetize your kitchen," I said. "K is for kindness."

Laura shot me a sharp look.

"And P can be for Pyramids," I added, "as a nod to our source."

I stood in the doorway while she divided cucumber slices and red pepper strips onto a million plates. Children of all ages sniffed my form there and, like hungry sentries, pushed me aside to assure themselves of free passage through the castle gate.

"Go," Laura would say each time, to mine and her own. "I'll tell you when dinner is ready."

"G is for little Godots," I offered.

Laura didn't hear me. She was off into her own kitchen alphabet.

"I'll tell you what A stands for," she said. "A is for anger, and it all goes downhill from there."

This is Laura's kitchen alphabet:

Anger, Accomplish, Annoy
Bother, Broil, Boil, Boring, Blank, Buttered
Chop, Catastrophe in the making, Choice
Duty, Devoid, Danger, Dagger, Defenseless
Entertain, Escape, Empty, Endless
Frustration, Fast
Grudgingly
Hurry, Hate, Hinder, Helpless, Hopeless, Harmless, History
Imagination, Incapable, Insult, Inhibit, Insecure
Justifiable, Judgment
Kitchen, Kaplan
Labor, Long, Late, Lose, Listen
Mystery, Mom, Mind
Negotiation, No win
Orders, Opinionated, Obligation
Picky
Questions, Quell, Quick
Recipe, Ripe, Reason, Regular
Slave, Stifled, Shopping, Small, Slow, Satisfy, Struggle
Terror, Tedious, Tight, Tasteless, Torture
Undeserved
Variation
Wary, Win
X
Yield
Zero

"Not too many foods in there." I smiled.
"I don't cook," said Laura.

"A is for Apple?"

"Anger," Laura said.

"Who's the mom?" I asked.

"Don't ask."

I didn't ask about the K for Kaplan either, although it moved me more than the other words, because it was her maiden name, and it had arrived in her kitchen alphabet like a long-lost friend, like someone you don't know well anymore, could be very wrong about, but loved once and wanted to love again. Her words were accusations that Ping-Ponged between children, husband, and self. I knew who Picky was, who Won, who Struggled, who at the end of twenty-six roads landed at Zero.

"Z is for Zen," I offered. "Life's 'supreme meal' cooked up in your kitchen."

"That would be nice."

The phone rang and it fell into her neck like the kiss of a lover. I was left alone, inches from Laura but miles from her thoughts, listening to her sort out a problem at her museum— a children's museum she helped to found and was now help- ing to run. Whenever I have brought a telephone into our kitchen at home, my children suddenly find a reason to howl, pull themselves from a game or book, and swarm over me with demands until I can no longer hear the voice in the re- ceiver. The kitchen is sacred, a place in which only they might star. I remember the feeling, the perfect comfort there, the absence of fears. Oh, the creatures under my bed. Oh, the monsters in the closet and the boogeymen in the attic and the Things in the basement, but nothing frightening ever lived in the kitchen.

When Laura put down the receiver, she apologized. Then it rang again.

Laura had worked in real estate before the children came along. It was lucrative. It was easy. But motherhood had worked its naked magic and Laura needed more meaningful work. She got involved with the creation of the children's museum, flung heart and soul into its labored success, and eventually was asked to become the deputy director. The pay wasn't much, and that wasn't without importance, but it was critical to Laura to have a job that gave her a sense of intellectual worth and dignity. Real estate hadn't done it.

Because Laura had committed herself to so much undoing: undoing the childhood in Los Angeles and the cheap easy that availed itself there; undoing a mother lying exhausted on the couch, because her father had left them early and her mother worked nights to support the two girls; undoing the first marriage; undoing the emptiness of her childhood kitchen; undoing the lack of self-worth that seemed to emerge from it all like a bad odor drifting out of the stockpot.

Tell her to go back to real estate for the money and she would turn savage, not to you, because she knew you were thinking of the family's needs, but to herself, for prioritizing her sense of worth over the finances. Tell her the pasta salad wasn't worth the effort, and she might sear you with her pain, because no one had ever tried to make her nice meals each evening, and she knew the value of it, and she despised the mean oblivion of affluence. Laura had been undoing the first twenty-odd years, unraveling the yarn that trailed from Los Angeles to New York, and picking out the bits of hay. She had formed cautious ties with the past, but she had not taken a shears to them, which was a credit to her strength. It took much of her strength.

And then there were moments of toppling, because fighting the past consumed her energies, spent her patience and isolated her, like the midday sun without even a shadow to cast around it. She cried rarely. She would call me in moments of anguish and let the telephone be the confessional, her mouth to my ear with no distraction of faces, no visual testimony of despair. When she spoke, her voice choked and breaking off, I felt around me the blackness of a crypt at night.

"Do you have a minute?" she would whisper, drinking the tears that fell backward into her throat. They dropped in the slow chosen words of her narrations. Plunk, Plunk came the recounting of the story, the pain which constricted her throat, the disbelief that life disappointed the way it did, that mothers continued not to understand, that husbands continued to be mute or opaque, that children didn't trust your guidance, that your guidance was poor.

"Call her back," I once said, when Laura's mother had perpetrated the hurt, unconsciously, consciously, trying to give Laura a gift, knowing that a stack of bills left behind on her bureau was the wrong way. I wasn't pushing Laura to be magnanimous but I had a soft spot for reconciliations with mothers while they're alive.

We stood facing each other in her kitchen. Laura looked at me with astonishment. Maybe it wasn't astonishment, but rage. I couldn't tell. The air between us was transparent, but it might've come from over the Andes and rushed upward with rains and freezing temperatures that seemed desperate for Canada, racing between us in that tiny kitchen, making it impossible to see her clearly.

"Don't let the incident sit through history without a dialogue," I murmured, because so many incidents sit lonely, without words to soothe and describe, without jeering grotesqueries in the marginalia. They look bigger on the page that way, when they are so unhistoric really, one pebble in a gravel path. I could not picture Laura's mother, back in Los Angeles now, not cooking, not reading, not near her daughters, not remarried. I could only see her second daughter, a small stone ripping the sole of her foot.

I said, "There is a kind of loneliness ahead." There in the dim obscurity of a woman's future, the living longer, the impossibility of dying before all those fragile towers of dignity crumble. Will I be posited in a nursing home, forgotten by my grandchildren and their children, bereft of my husband and muttering, "Laura, Laura," as though she were there with me in those last days of life when there is only a bed and a strongbox, when early memories of childhood scurry up around the mind like lost children, and the past seems so much more alive than the present, and hasn't it always?

*"I long / to be with you where angels dream / of ginghams in the lily-spangled dawn."*

Laura plucked herself from her irritation.

"I'm writing a poem," I said.

"About your mother? She didn't believe in angels."

"She believed in writing poems while cooking."

*Up in the endless ethers, congeries*
*of angels swing pendulous scrolls*
*from the gated keep of Elysium. Peter*

*greets arriving souls, vetoes*
*cloud-sown chrysanthemums for the old*
*verbena borders by his pearly threshold.*

"A fussy Peter," I grinned. "Are you laughing?"
"Not yet," Laura said.

*God is away, as always, galling*
*another planet with ambiguous prose,*
*when you appear, contused, smaller*

*than registered, unscheduled, distressed,*
*still unshed of the one-dimensional*
*hospital dress.*

"She would rather have arrived in blue pumps, you know, and
a proper dress from Bonwit's."

*Unsightly, you felt*

*at first, as though you would fail*
*to make good-bye more graceful. But later,*
*as cancer rained its scandal hail,*

*you smiled and surrendered your own*
*trial of senses to its tireless final*
*say. You seemed relieved, bone-*

*weary of breathing, never expecting*
*a wide-open hereafter. Fatigue*
*blisters the crystalline steps where*

*memories smooth carbuncular regrets*
*from the amber skin of infant death.*
*You weep to learn eternity is left.*

"Are you crying yet?" I asked.
"Just about."
"It's difficult, searching for the poetic icon while you chop root
vegetables for a roast."

*The meadows sweet with every conceivable*
*clover leave you cold. They need*
*no weeding. Morning glories weave*

*their leafy muscle unlaboriously up*
*the mullioned golden trellises that lean*
*immortally on nought. Once at dusk,*

*as I scrubbed beans in a distant sink,*
*the rubble of a battered breeze crumbled*
*at my feet, like a painful sigh that linked*

*our lonely monologues. I long*
*to be with you where angels dream*
*of ginghams in the lily-spangled dawn.*

"I'm crying now," whispered Laura.

"It could have been leeks," I reflected. " 'As I scrubbed leeks . . . ' All that sand. But the K was too hard."

"K is for kitchen," Laura said. "It's in my alphabet."

⁓

One hot summer day I took my children to the playground a block from Laura's apartment. We were to wait for her there, and then we would go to her place for a dinner of pasta and corn salad.

"You boil the pasta. You open the jar . . ." Laura had said when I accused her of cooking.

It was a fine plan, only I was nearly faint by the time we reached her apartment, splashed water from the kitchen sink on my face, and caught my breath sitting on the trash can.

"This is a sanctuary for me," I said, looking up at her from the garbage lid. She seemed more bewildered than worried.

"A sanctuary?" Laura asked, throwing a sharp glance in an arc over the stained stove coils, and a glass pitcher in which knives and forks and spoons were splayed, noosed, like an ugly bouquet. Our children were making unastounding noises from the four corners of her apartment while she found cups with tops and cups without tops for water, juice, juice combinations, and water and juice combinations, because children become particular quickly about one of the few things over which they are given dominion, and so be it: The Drink. Laura had taken drink orders and sent them off to disassemble mounds of toys that sat like mesas across an ancient waterbed of carpeted floor.

Relief was being away from the playground, its hot and foreign busyness that might as well have been downtown Cairo for the

195

way I had to watch my children, the unpredictable traffic of other humans and their children, their shouts like horns honking, mounting my spine and gradually cementing my vertebrae with mild anxiety. There wasn't a drinking fountain in sight and I couldn't walk without sinking into the deep sand that gave none of the pleasures of its cousin, the beach, but instead dusted up about my face like ill magic with each screaming pass of the bigger boys; and where was Maddie but there, partaking of another child's abandoned shovel and pail; and where was Hugh but there, at the top of some spiraling slide; so I leaned against the diaper bag, that precious sack of life-sustaining sundries, as though it were the axis of our survival there on that broad bustling playground, our sack of gold pieces in the wilderness. It was a wasteland of drought, clamor, and unrelated rocketing bodies.

"It was only a playground," Laura said. "Find a bench and compose another poem."

"There are periods of great vulnerability in life, when everything outside my house seems desolate, populated by hostile strangers. Then I find myself here in your kitchen and I feel like I have found safety and love."

"Because when you're in your own kitchen, you're surrounded by things you need to do. When you're in somebody else's kitchen, there's nothing for you to do. And in my kitchen," she laughed, "there's no room for anybody to do anything."

She had found us at the playground. She had ambled toward the swings carrying a bottle of water, casually reviewing the other mothers the way the hydra's head turns floatily in the water to find food drifting by; because this was Laura's playground, and she walked through it as if she were hosting a cocktail party, nodding to the lesser known, pausing with old friends, finding me, the outsider in her space, and bringing me water, which I needed before I knew it. She laughed when I told her that's how I perceived her, that she breathed an air of assurance and calm. Laura perceived herself more along the lines of those treacherous inlets off the coast of Newfoundland, in which even the sea life perishes in the violent froth. Not exactly a safe harbor, she might have said.

"That's nice," she said instead, smiling at the irony, at the great sea-floor trench that had been carved away by the diluvial waters of time between private self and public self, between the little girl and the mother she becomes, between our securities and our demons, between the things we share among friends and the things we never share.

Laura always let me make of her what I needed. She never interfered with my insistence that she be the storybook sea that promised to carry my boat to safe shores. You could rely on her. She was always waiting for the child disembarking a school bus. She was always there at the hospital, pacing the corridors with you in early labor. She always found a telephone when you were in a moment of peeled vulnerability. There was always a warm dinner on the table by six, no matter what comments greeted it.

"I would like to be a sanctuary," she said, without a sigh of sentiment, but with sentiment, too aware that life needed painting and touching up, and wouldn't it have been better if nothing needed cosmetics; and wasn't it the task of the mother to make life look nice, feel nice, taste nice, and then be the one who walked the child into the harsh world despairing that she couldn't make it nicer.

"Jane Eyre," I said, "walked starving out of the wilderness into the 'humble kitchen' of what proved to be her cousins."

Laura eyed me. "Are you starving?"

"No. But kitchens are notoriously welcoming. They are hearths. Playgrounds are wildernesses," I added.

"I see," she said, not giving an inch.

"Jane Eyre saw the warm glow of candlelight and fireplace. It pierced the horrible night."

Laura gazed up at her light fixture. A bulb had blown and through the frosted glass it appeared as a dull gray blotch, like the gloomy shadow of a cancer mass on an X-ray film.

"Maybe I should install candles in the new kitchen and call it a hearth," Laura said. "Fewer people would expect meals to emerge from it."

"And you could dump twenty tons of gravel on your lawn and not have to cut it," I offered.

Laura considered. "I could make stone soup."

I had to find the story in my head. When I did, I wrinkled my nose. "Stone soup depends on wringing ingredients from stupid stingy neighbors."

Laura sighed. "Find me a new fairy tale."

"A woman knew a story," I began. "She also knew a song. But she kept them to herself, never told anyone the story or sang the song. Imprisoned within her, the story and the song were feeling choked. They wanted release. They wanted to run away. One day, when she was sleeping with her mouth open, the story escaped, fell out of her, took the shape of a little boy and sat at her kitchen table. The song also escaped, took the shape of a little girl and pulled at her refrigerator door. They were there in her kitchen when she woke up. They were hungry and loved what she cooked them. They were sleepy and napped while she stroked their hair. They were frightened and found comfort in her embrace.

"The woman's husband came home, looked at the little boy and girl and asked his wife, 'Who is visiting?'

" 'No one,' she said.

" 'Whose children are these?'

" 'I don't know,' she replied.

"He wasn't satisfied with her answer. He was suspicious. Their conversation was unpleasant. The unpleasantness led to a quarrel. The husband flew into a rage, picked up his blanket, and went to a neighbor's house to sleep.

"The woman didn't understand what had happened. She lay down alone that night. She asked the same question over and over: 'Whose little boy and girl are these?' Baffled and unhappy, she put out her lamp and went to sleep.

"Every evening all the birds of the village would gather together to sing in the dark. That night they gathered in a tree outside the window where the husband slept. All the birds were singing and whispering except one, a finch, who came late.

"The birds asked the finch, 'Why are you so late tonight?'

" 'I was listening to a couple quarreling,' said the finch.

" 'Why did they quarrel?'

" 'While the husband was at work, a little boy and a little girl appeared in the kitchen and were hungry and wanted to be nur-

199

tured. The husband came home and wanted to know whose children they were that his wife was caring for so dearly. The wife said she didn't know. So they quarreled.'

" 'But where did the children come from?'

" 'The woman of this house knew a story and a song. She has never told the story, and has never sung the song. The story and the song were being suffocated inside; so they escaped through her mouth as she was sleeping and turned into a little boy and a little girl.'

"The husband, lying under his blanket beside the open window, heard the finch's explanation. His suspicions were cleared. At dawn, he went home and asked his wife about her story and her song. But she had forgotten both of them.

" 'What story, what song?' she said."

Laura stared at me. She didn't speak for a long time. Then she said, "I hope your story and your song like corn salad."

## *Laura's Corn Salad*

| | |
|---|---|
| 4 ears fresh corn, cooked, kernels carved into a big bowl | Chopped cucumber |
| | Chopped green onions |
| | 3 tablespoons mirin |
| | 1 tablespoon soy sauce |
| Chopped red pepper | 3 tablespoons sesame oil |

"No lemongrass?" I asked.

Laura smiled. "There are spice packets for people like you."

Laura's new house had many rooms. Some were cheerful, but the kitchen was dilapidated and depressing. She didn't want me to see it. She was mildly ashamed of it, of owning it, of having herself briefly reflected in its dingy mirror.

"It's vintage fifties," she said. "They only made macaroni and cheese back then. Wait until it's gone."

Most kitchens are not the sunlit cafés of tidy bounty that one is subjected to on glistening magazine covers. They tend to be small and unrenovated. The Formica, a fat flower pattern, curls in the corners the way mums dry up and go brown in October; there's a black hole on the countertop the size of a cigarette burn, with a scorch flaring off like a comet's trail where *he* put down the pot without thinking. The oven door shuts like a tin toy and inside there are charcoal splotches everywhere because no one cleans it, because somebody's too old, or doesn't see very well, can't bend to do it. The sink is stainless steel with stains. The refrigerator is dark and the freezer is in the garage, which is why the car is on the lawn. There's not much counter space, but you don't need much for macaroni from a box. There's a little table and two metal chairs. A wooden plaque on the wall says Bless My Kitchen and in the window hanging from a suction cup is a faux stained glass of a sailboat and another of a seagull. Little porcelain creatures clog the windowsill and a blue window shade with fringe hasn't been pulled in years. The wallpaper has silver metallic lines in it. The knives bend when you try to cut a squash. The stirring spoons are plastic, the dishwasher is useless, the linoleum is gritty, and the room will smell forever of the morning's coffee.

*She* has a subscription to some gourmet magazine, and while he watches the television every night, she flips through wildly complicated recipes for crème caramel and Thai noodles and huevos rancheros, because it is somehow relaxing and pleasing to imagine making things, to see your fingers at the tip of the knife, mincing scallions, deveining shrimp, whisking eggs into custard so deftly; never mind the arthritis, or that he always crinkled his nose above a plate of something new, and what do you do with all the extra lemon curd, anyway, because you only need two tablespoons for the recipe? Their children are grown and gone, and no one did Thanksgiving the way Mom did, so each year they try to re-create the whole Plymouth plantation in their own kitchens, kitchens with Looks—hers country, his wife's French provincial, both cheap knockoffs, adulterated versions, but clean, packed with appliances from a store being sued for unfair hiring practices; and the offspring, the F1 generation, are now pouring jars of pearl onions into a canned broth, remembering how they helped Mom put marshmallows on top of the sweet potatoes, even though they didn't, because she wouldn't let them.

That was the kitchen Laura bought and would be renovating so that no one would recognize it. Laura felt defined by this room she hated, and maybe it was true that we are better defined by what we hate than what we love, but the problem was: Laura didn't hate cooking, she only hated cooking unappreciated. The process of remodeling forced her to pick out her instruments of torture, the color of her cell walls.

"The burners have a thirty-degree tilt," Laura said. "First your eggs slop down to one edge of the pan, then they burn."

She was trying to describe it to me—not the yard, not the living room, not the bedrooms, but the house according to the kitchen. The kitchen was the axis on which the whole house spun.

Later, "We're adding a pantry," she said, with satisfied cheer, as though she'd just added the teaspoon of tarragon that perfected her soup.

The kitchen. It's the room that materializes from a child's memory and begs re-creation—the scents of promising pies, the issuing of warm nourishment, the pure pleasure of its bounty, and the mother waiting there to delight you with a new taste. It is like the staging of a child's favorite story. We conjure images of hot ovens, splashy sinks, baskets of onions and potatoes, bins of fresh bread, fleshy women with merry faces.

Like a tedious tradition we pore over pages of recipes with glorious pictures, although our images have all had to diet down, and we mothers are supposed to be doling out fresh green beans instead of buns to slim exemplars of rosy-cheeked children. Kitchen magazines in four-color zeal show us how to line the reed basket from Bali with a French dish towel and set it, towering with kumquats from a commune of Asian gardeners near San Destin, just so; the copper pot hung, just so; the green glass pitcher in the middle of the island butcher block, just so, until finally we sack the antediluvian order of our countertops, step by step, with a barrage of onion skins, a siege of measuring spoons, a frightening cloud of flour, and the thunder of a slammed oven door. Then comes the flood. The sink runs for an hour while we try to clean up the mess, scrape off the flour-and-water paste, and rinse ourselves of sweat and food dusts.

⟳

The move to Laura's new house was imminent, and when I lingered in her kitchen she was more often preparing forms than meals.

The general contractor asked her whether she wanted a raised patisserie surface. People who made lots of pies and breads and tarts, he said, preferred a higher counter. It was easier on the back.

"I don't bake," Laura said.

The supplier suggested two dishwashers. Laura was intrigued. She tried to do a kind of math that would give her one-half the dirty dishes, or double the interval between unloadings. I said nothing. My image of hell is a small kitchen with two sinks of dirty dishes and two dishwashers full of clean dishes that need to be unloaded. Forget the fires and the disemboweling. You spend eternity loading and unloading the dishwasher, and while you might like to go crazy doing it, because insanity would take the edge off the horror, you don't. You're not allowed to go crazy in hell. Otherwise it wouldn't be torment.

The architect asked Laura what kind of refrigerator she wanted. She gave him what sounded like a license plate number, because she had done her research, because that kind of work came easy to her, as easy as title searches and real estate closings; and then she fumed that men were the lucky pirates of society, as though the tangled work of mothering were ill-luck.

"Maybe you should get into the business of kitchen remodeling," I sighed, finally taking the bait.

"No," snapped Laura. "I just want to be acknowledged, or better, paid for motherhood." She clicked her pen tip in and out
of its sheath. In Morse Code it ticked out: R-E-S-P-E-C-T [stop]
D-I-S-T-A-N-C-E.

"Did you know that kitchen counters are three feet tall?" Laura
said, but her words made a vain line of communication, like the
dribble of water trickling from her broken faucet.

"I never asked myself," I said.

"You've asked yourself every other question."

A slight hung there between us. We eyed each other, two
friends who had grown closer over time in spite of every difference
in our natures, aware that friends could sustain the complemen-
tarities the way a husband and wife could not, could love one
another year after year without the erosion of opposites in proximity. It was a simple ground rule of coexistence that cemented
us over time, so that we needn't always understand each other,
needn't pass judgment. That was the generous life force of friendship: That there was space. But friendship still took work and
relied on overlooking this and that, and could grow faint when
the space was too vast, because space could become a geograph-
ical force diminishing mile by mile the strength of the web spun
between two hearts.

We were feeling vulnerable and wounded. We both retreated.
I wandered off with a book about kitchen tiles while she set the
kettle to boil.

I was glad it was not my kitchen to determine. The business
of renovation was too much like the mirror held to your head
after a haircut. It continued to reflect you too closely, from every

angle, spelling out to architect and contractor and beautician alike your most intimate wrinkles.

I don't do that.

You don't?

I prefer this.

You do?

I need a Lazy Susan for assembling my poisons.

Of course.

Laura said, "I need a radio in the kitchen so I can think about books and politics while I'm doing what I hate with my hands."

Hurrah for you, my mother would have said. A woman was obligated to make it work for herself, because no one else was going to lift a finger. But the architect had flickered with irritation. He designed for cheerful outcomes.

"A woman is stripped in the kitchen," Laura said, handing me a cup of hot tea and settling herself with the same nearby. "Not in the way a man would like her to be, but stripped of all her identifying signs, stripped of her professionalism. She is naked."

"I like that kind of nakedness," I protested. "I like a place where bracelets are for falling into soups. I like the idea that nice perfume gets pounced upon, strangled and stomped on by the scent of roast lamb."

My mind raced on. I liked, in the kitchen, feeling stripped to the senses, so that I could better hear the sizzling of garlic in the pan, better see the brilliance of a blood orange on winter's blanched palate, better taste the singular seeds of a pomegranate, better feel the leek's sheaf of papers scrolled into a baton, better smell the promise of cookies as they first melt down, then inflate.

"Ode to a Kitchen?" Laura asked, watching me.

"Ode to a Scullerymaid," I laughed.

"Still, suffragette after suffragette?"

I said, "I have pounded cold butter sticks into batter since I was a child. When I do it now, I have a keen inkling of who I am, my core. Or at least, I know who I am not."

I was not a poor Irish waif, destined for the mad hand of an impoverished and drunken father, one of eight, bold-eyed children, daring the camera to name me as the one who took the candy from the barrel.

I was not a Chesapeake crabber, hands barnacled with calluses and smelling always of salt and the blood of triumphant kills, crooked as a fish hook from hauling traps out of the heavy sucking water and into my boat for too little money and no worth.

I was not of royal blood, a glider through halls too wide and shined, my eyes resting regally on mantel clocks and my hands too smooth for the rough edges of a cheese.

Laura cleared her throat with impatience. For her, questions and answers were arrows shot at close targets, with minimal arcs, minimal earth-spin, minimal wind resistance. I was arc, spin, and resistance gathered into one. I was distraction on two feet.

"Who are you?" she asked.

"I am short," I grinned. "To me, all countertops are patisserie surfaces. Who are you?"

Laura thought. Tea was for reflecting. Tea was for reflecting with company. Tea sipped alone was just wet.

She said with a shrug, "I'm angry."

Kitchen sinks surrounded by Delft tiles fell away in front of me and I saw only a photograph album that began with the wedding of her parents and progressed like a ladder of sunny patches to Laura's beau and on to Laura's wedding and then her two children. There was Laura in her parent's faces and her children's smiles, and always her own eyes staring at the photographer with uncertainty, as though she was caught there between her past and her future, the one she wanted to renounce and the other she wanted to shape; and nothing had been exactly as she had meant it to be, and she could never control it, never.

She said, "I'm angry because I will never know the feeling of going into my kitchen and preparing something satisfying and putting it on the table and having people eat it and say thank you. It won't happen. How do you move from that spot?"

I couldn't answer.

"Anger keeps me from being a nicer person than I want to be. And even that makes me angry."

We were quiet. I let my eyes wander down to the book of kitchen tiles like two balloons left to drift soundlessly from the heavens to bump-POP upon the earth.

"Listen," I said. "I had this dream. I dreamed that the doctors would give my first baby back to me alive, but only for a short while. Everyone cautioned me against it. They told me that if I were to have her alive, it would destroy me afresh when she was taken away again. Everyone pleaded with me to think it over. They were fervently against it. I accused them of asking the wrong questions and ran outside to be alone.

"I took a walk up the mountain to a small house where an old man lived. He was a very old man with many books on his walls and staggery stacks of books that rose up from his old Persian carpet, first to the left and then to the right, but never toppling. He was examining something at his table, with a bare bulb over his bald and wrinkled head. I told him my dilemma.

" 'You will feel her die, in your arms,' he said, without lifting his old head from his work. 'You will feel her turn cold.'

" 'I need to see her again,' I said.

" 'That's always how we feel about people who have died.'

" 'I need her to know that I was there to hold her on the other side of birth.'

" 'You think she doesn't know that already?'

"Then, something in his work startled him and with silver tweezers he lifted carefully what looked to be a sliver of paper up to the weak bulb.

"I squinted toward the soft light to see what he saw.

"He said, 'You can't save her. You could do nothing the first time. You can do nothing this time.' "

" 'I understand that,' I said. But he had made me doubtful now.

" 'Look at this,' said the old man, and he waved his silver tweezers toward me. A small swatch of paper, yellow and orange and pink, fluttered like gossamer in the light. Suddenly the bulb became brighter and I could see the very weave of paper, the ripped edges, and the filaments of fiber reaching out into the cold air where they had been torn.

" 'It's very old,' I heard the old man say, from somewhere, as though he were whispering through the hole in the sky where this little patch of dawn had been snatched.

" 'Where is it from?' I asked, caught in its spell.

" 'From the East. From abandoned military outposts in the mountains, where the monks went to gaze outward in meditation. They made the finest paper on which to write their stories of Buddha, thousands of years old. Look closely. There is writing on this small piece.'

"I looked harder. A tracery of ink I hadn't seen before emerged against the paper's celestial glow.

" 'What does it say?' I whispered.

"The old man said, in a faraway voice that shivered through valleys too broad for mountains to encompass, 'Don't relive life.' "

Laura took a cautious sip of tea.

"Meaning?" she said, although she knew already, that we can learn little but be reminded of much, that there is pain from love, and art from anguish, and wisdom from suffering.

*March on.*

I said, "Control. Repetition. Distraction. We have no control. We repeat the bad as well as the good. We need to be distracted from ourselves. And," I added, "don't forget to hire a feng shui master to bless your new kitchen."

Laura was blinking, a lot.

I said, "Women say 'excuse me,' when they sneeze, and men say 'eh.' "

She laughed, and my heart started beating again.

She tapped her pen against her knee. "The contractor wants to put old pine boards on the kitchen floor," she sighed. "He's got a supplier, a guy who tears down old barns."

"That's a lot of baggage for a kitchen floor," I said. *Whoops.* "But I'm sure it's attractive—an old wavy wood floor."

Laura smiled tenderly. "The world looks wavy to me," she said. "Because I've got tears in my eyes."

## *Fifteen Years Later: Laura's Autobiography*

*My first marriage taught me that if you're going to get out, do it fast. Or maybe it was my father who taught me, before I was looking for the tip. He left when I was three.*

*My second marriage has always been on the precipice, but I have never woken up wanting a divorce. The fights simmer for years and the resentment layers, but still I don't want a divorce. We have two children who cemented us into a family. We both love them uncondi- tionally. Maybe the marriage would have been happier childless, but that's old snow.*

*I didn't divorce my husband. I can't divorce my children. By the time they were in high school, I had to face them amplified by adoles- cence, their crew of shuffling friends, their sullen faces a constant reminder of my failures as a mother and wife. I'd given it my best shot, which may not have been much. I wondered why they kept coming home, why they didn't lose themselves to friends' houses, or after-school programs. They slunk through the kitchen door, day after day after school day, in the same way my husband came home, night after night, to reiterate his grievances, to balk about dinner. Me, too, I suppose. I just stayed on, not packing my bags and leaving, but not ready to put one more penny in the slot. We had made our misery from scratch, and we were invested in it.*

*That's when I put fresh lightbulbs in the barn. First it was just to* read out there, beyond the noises of dissatisfaction in the house. I brought out a stack of books and lay them in the wheelbarrow. I dragged in an old easy chair from the basement, and a table.

It felt like an empty cathedral although it was only a little barn, one dilapidated room and one tiny bathroom. We'd always used it as a potting shed, as a place to store bicycles in the winter. I hadn't really looked at it for years. Light streamed through the big barn doors and the demi-door of the hay loft where the former owner had put large glass panels. There was power and plumbing because he had used it as a woodworking shop. There was sawdust where you might have looked for wisps of straw.

I read out there and it seemed like the first time in my whole life— white streaking through my black hair like a hostile takeover, creases deep across my face—that I had a moment's peace. The quiet. The quiet hit me like a frying pan. No televisions. No whining overaged children. The quiet was more like company than my family had ever been. It encouraged me. I began to paint. After all those years of working in a museum, my hands seemed to be recalling what my eyes had seen.

I bought a thermos, a mug, and a dish towel. Out came a plate one day with a sandwich on it, and it never went back to the kitchen where my children were complaining about the dishes in the sink and the never-there mother. They thought I was going mad. I caught them once peeking into our bedroom for signs that I wasn't sleeping in the house at night. I caught my daughter checking my closet to see if I'd moved clothes. It was their imagination that prodded me. I moved a cot into the barn. They said nothing. I kept fresh flowers in a vase on the floor by the glass doors. Layers of sweaters and pants accumulated in a heap in a corner. I lined a shelf on the wall with plates, cups, and silverware.

When I bought a small refrigerator and a toaster oven I got a call from the school guidance counselor.

"Your children are worried," she said. "They say you've moved out of the house."

"I'm in the backyard," I said.

"Children," she sighed academically. "Children need their mothers at home."

"I didn't leave them," I said. I didn't leave them as infants, I didn't leave them for another woman. I helped my daughter get on the pill. I went to my son's soccer matches and spelled out the need for precautions. I never said "You're too young," or "Shame on you."

"You're there and you're not," said the counselor, her voice phrasing what her mind could not.

"I'm not a goblin."

"Who is cooking them dinner?" she asked.

"They have a liberated father," I answered. I wanted to tell her about my own father, who liberated himself when I was just learning to speak. Then I didn't speak for a year. I woke up one morning when I was four years old and broke my silence by saying, "There are no little bunnies anymore."

But the guidance counselor didn't care. "They are still children," she pleaded. "Sometimes, with adolescents, we forget."

We forget with adults, too, I thought. I said, "My children have dabbled in all aspects of adulthood except maturity." I heard myself say it, there, in a barn with a phone; a half-baked flight from the family, a nice example of maturity.

She cleared her throat. "Is there much fighting in the house?"

I said, "Not anymore."

We both knew a period had been put on this sentence, a varnish on our conversation, because there had been so much fighting for so long, and it occupied our house like a toxic ozone, smothering all other forms of life.

I had an urge to defend myself. After all, at least one of us was content now. I could have told the guidance counselor that I was painting well, understanding what I read, enjoying food, even enjoying cooking for myself. It was lonely enjoying life, suddenly, with nobody to tell. But it was nice, too—nobody there to complain about scallions in a sauce, or cabbage not cooked to perfect softness, nobody grumbling that it needed salt. The sound of frying peppers was pleasing when it wasn't competing with the television. The oven fan was calming. I started painting produce, painting it whole and sliced and crowded round with other things. I was reveling in a new love of foodstuffs. I was a born-again kitchen-woman.

After a couple of months my daughter came in and sat quietly with me while I painted. Her shoes were wet from the backyard grass, but she said nothing, which raised her inestimably in my admiration. I made us both a cup of hot coffee and in silence we looked through the big glass doors at a plain sight: A patch of unmown lawn, scrub trees, a swatch of other houses. Life was plain like that, not the fairy tale I'd read to her when she was tiny and lay in bed in footed pajamas surrounded by a junta of dolls and animals. I was plain, too, which was always an unflattering illumination for a child and its mother.

She had tried to make her world so wide, so fast, and it hadn't worked. I didn't blame her for trying. But what a surprise to glance up and find your road is going nowhere. You look behind you and there's your mother in the backyard barn, removing herself from whatever wretched normalcy the family had created. Maybe the barn looked suddenly like a safe house.

My daughter sat there with me, and we breathed each other's air and found some shared forgiveness. Her need for me was my grace.

She began to come regularly and I always put down my paints when she arrived. One day she turned up with some sort of chicken glop she'd cooked on her own. "Goulash," she called it. That became her code word for chopping up anything she found and throwing it into our big blue stew pot. She told me how much fun she had making it. Her brother and father had eaten it. Providing dinner made her feel strong.

"Is that silly?" she whispered.

"No. It's not silly," I assured her.

Her face was alive, shy, beautiful.

"What happened?" she asked me, waving a long arm through the barn.

"I don't know," I said. "The Chinese had typewriters two thousand years ago. Sometimes we lose hold of things for a while and have to rediscover them."

"Love?"

"Maybe not love itself, but its body of laws and principles."

"Love is a science?" she laughed.

"Love," I said, "is a method."

I bought a huge enamel stove and had it installed in the barn. It looked silly there, in its immensity. But it was beautiful. Green with copper fixtures. I did it for my daughter, my little girl. I wanted to make an overture from my world to hers. She loved it. She spent her afternoons with me, cooking while I painted. I don't remember ever being so happy.

*She dragged her brother out to the barn to have dinner with us, and he seemed surprised to find me at peace there, not blowing fire from my nose. Boredom at home had propelled him into a summer job—a beacon of initiative I couldn't have foreseen. Meanwhile, my husband hung out a new shingle and began practicing divorce law. It was lucrative, he mumbled at me one day. He'd come out to the barn at last. He didn't want to serve me papers, he said. He'd gotten to know divorce firsthand and it was worse than having a wife in the barn.*

*My daughter is a chef now. My son is in dental school. He complains that we never paid attention to his overbite. And I'm selling my paintings to cafés and gourmet food stores. I shake my head with wonder every time they give me the money. When the children went off to college, I moved back into the house. Time devoured my rancor. Time softened my husband's needs. It's all I ever wanted to do—paint, love my children, stand by my husband.*

*We are all guilty of contributing to the pain of those around us. I know I'm not innocent. I won't suggest that I offered my children a good example of self-fulfillment. But the old rules weren't working anymore. I changed the rules to rescue myself, and I rescued us all.*

This is a recipe for shrimp and noodles from Laura's daughter, the chef.

## *Angel Hair Shrimp*

Sauté one small chopped onion in butter and oil until translucent. Add a clove's worth of minced garlic. Let sizzle 2 minutes. Add ½ cup of orange juice, ¼ cup of chopped parsley, 1 tablespoon dried basil, and some salt and pepper. Simmer to thickness. Add ½ teaspoon of lemon zest. Toss in 8 shelled shrimp and cook until pink, about 3 minutes to be safe (it depends on the size of your shrimp). Give it a good shake of Tabasco, stir well, and throw it over angel hair pasta. Serves 2 in a barn.

# 8

## *The Congregation*

MY MOTHER LOVED the old cemeteries. In western Massa-
chusetts they are scattered discreetly off roads that were once
main thoroughfares, now thin and sunken lines between grassy
embankments, like the stitch of a single gray thread across the
quilted earth. You could miss the gravestones if you weren't looking up, down, and off to the side.

My mother was always looking up, down, and off to the side,
so we would stumble on a small sleeping cemetery as she took me
to find wool in Deerfield, pick apples in Cummington, or to swim-
ming holes off Route 66. I would be home from kindergarten,
bundled into the passenger seat and taking in the adventure,
when she would spot a pool of gathered stones. She would make
a soft noise, brake suddenly, and ease the car onto the yielding
shoulder of the road.

"Do you mind if we stop a minute?" she asked. But the station wagon would have already ground to a halt. "Just a quick stop," she would smile, opening the passenger door to lift me out and help me across the hushed road.

She'd wander into the cemetery with a deepening quiet, each step distancing her from my whines. At the first gravestones, my hand was loosed and I would be free to find betterment among the toppling lichen-mottled stones and spiky grasses. I made Japanese fans from pine needles, hung on the pickets of the tilting wrought-iron gate, plumped heavily onto the ground and waited, and grumbled.

She would step among the shoulders of the gravestones, and it was clear that she was in no hurry. She'd read the names aloud, trace the prophetic inscriptions with a finger, and kneel, her stockinged knees nestled into twigs and earth, to brush the silts from the last rhyming word of warning, the last number of a date. She'd move from stone to stone, as a bee does from blossom to blossom, as though no James or William or With Wife Mary were to be missed. She dispensed remembrance: *I shall bear you in mind, you are not forgotten.*

Eventually my mother would find a tiny segregation of small stones irregularly embedded in the earth, each one like a plaque commemorating a bit of sod. They were the graves of infants and children. At times the headstone was only the size of her hand, which she would lay across it, warming it, where once tears darkened it or a small toy graced it, simple names engraved above the scarcely spanning dates. *Amy. John.* There my mother's tour ended, and she would kneel heavily, finally, into the pine needles and weep. She wept for the babies, beloved, helpless, not strong

219

enough to survive, fallen by the wayside. She who had borne five, wept for the others' having died.

My mother could lose a whole afternoon unexpectedly to an old cemetery. When she came home, she checked the kitchen cupboards for canned pears in syrup. Here is her pear salad, which she could make for seven, in ten minutes.

## Pear Salad

Lettuce leaves freshly
washed and patted dry
Cottage cheese
Canned pears in heavy
syrup

¼ cup mayonnaise
¼ teaspoon paprika
Salt and pepper to taste

Place lettuce leaves attractively on a plate and set a pear half, midsection upward, in the middle. Put a scoop of cottage cheese in the pear half. Whisk the mayonnaise and paprika into the pear syrup until the lumps disappear, and drizzle over the salad. Sweet, cool and refreshing.

Thirty-five years later I spotted a cemetery off the road. I wandered into it, wondering what had drawn my mother. Stands of tall dark pines delineated sections with such law that I imagined St. Peter could peer down and use them for reference. The paths were white gravel and there were gardeners digging round holes for shrubs and trees as though in competition with the rectangular trenches of the graveyard workers. A row of crabapple trees lay shrouded in burlap on the ground. They looked like captured birds, bound, to check their flight. When the landscapers unwrapped them, they opened their branches slowly and gently into fullness.

I walked with uncertainty, the itch of not belonging softly nagging. I ambled down a path of deep green holly bushes and somber rhododendrons, past marble angels and meditative figures, under mountain aspens with their bright yellow leaves and red berries. To avoid a line of mourners, I ducked through an arbor and found myself on a small square of lawn, hedged off from noise and breeze by thick boxwood, removed from the vista of headstones. The shrubs were petite and burned in late fall colors of burnished metals. There were no statues, no benches. When I looked across the lush grass for a place to sit, I saw them: little white stones set into the green earth. Here were the graves of infants, like lily pads in a green reflecting pool.

I pushed blades of grass from around a stone that had only a name on it: *Elizabeth*. I touched my fingertips to the cool marble. Around her lay *Daniel, Ethan, Sarah, Brad, Christine*. Some of the infants had dates inscribed and I began calculating the ages. Two days for Sarah. Three months for Daniel. But Elizabeth had no day engraved below her name, no hyphen to bridge a moment of joy and hope with the moment of sorrow and loss, no span of hours. She was for all time, buried in the darkness she had always and only known.

And the tears came as though they had waited. I sobbed as I

knelt before the little stone, for my little girl and Elizabeth and Ethan and Brad and for all the babies in that somewhere crèche, without cries, without hunger.

A groan reached up from within me. "Mama," I wept. "Are you just surrounded there by babies?"

I sat for an hour by the small white stones. This green enclosure through the low arbor—it was a nursery for the mothers left behind.

It began to snow. Somewhere in that first white dust of winter, its blousy lazy horizontal sway back and forth, was the incontrovertible suggestion of death. As I stood at the kitchen sink, my hands under cold running water, I thought of those lost to wars and disease, whose souls seemed woefully alive in the unalighting flakes, unable to settle and rest. I set my mother warm above the white cloud-cover with my firstborn in her lap, and I felt at times that between them there was more of me up there than there was down here; here, in a gradually warming kitchen washing the ice from frozen blueberries in the breaking dark of dawn so that the household would be swollen with the scent of fresh muffins for breakfast.

Hugh padded into the kitchen in his socks and pajamas and sweatshirt, the last because he moved as much by night as by day and couldn't find his blankets in the midst of his grand pirate dreams. His face was puffy with sleep, teetering on that fence of moods, where one touch could push him into a rosy hug or a snoozy crabby scream of need—what need? Oh, but there was always a hairline gap that needed grouting.

Such was the morning. Dawn. Snow. Death. And then the arrival of this first angel, a tummy ferried about this world on two socked feet. How delicately he kept himself between options as he stood just inside the kitchen doorway. It was clear to me why kitchens had so many doorways. Children were always turning up there, red from play, or tearstained from a scolding, instant stalagmites each time you swung around, as if the kitchen were the endpoint of all their invisible passageways. They were mine or they were someone else's. Often enough I would look up to find a neighbor's child whimpering at the glass because he was running away from home.

I ran away a time or two myself, and looking back I wonder if there wasn't a conspicuous traffic up and down Harrison Avenue of little weeping children carrying a fresh pair of underpants and a toothbrush, dragging their toes along the sidewalks sluggishly, in case their mothers really did love them after all and would come running after them; but in case no mother came running, the child might flop on a neighbor's grassy lawn, return home, or find someone else's kitchen door, Mrs. Lee's, Mrs. Lundgren's, Mrs. Kiteley's. It happened mostly at dusk, in the summertime, when heat and fatigue melted the glue that usually kept things properly pasted—sharp words pasted in the mind, sweet words pasted on the tongue.

Now I was the mother down the block, the one with the big glass kitchen door through which little weepy runaways peered, to see if I was there, if my children were there, if I was maybe making those butterscotch brownies. They came with tiny shoulders sloping in exhaustion, the great exhaustion of sorrow, and when I clasped them in my arms, those shoulders seemed to mold to me as though their young bones were not yet flinty, as though they were soft-shelled children, vulnerable inside and out. They would show me their paper bag of fresh underwear and sometimes a comb to indicate how proper they were—tooth-brushers, hair-combers, but maligned, maligned, maligned. Their lower lips thrust forward like a dike against the tears as they told me of unfairness, of being unloved. I was moved that it was my door they came to in flight, that I had made this kitchen a safe place for them, that they accepted my brownies and my embrace although they wished with each sob it had been their own mothers who'd caught up with them, begging forgiveness. I was moved, too, that these children at five and six had already learned that we wanted to be loved in spite of ourselves, to be clasped not for our blackness but in spite of it, to be forgiven; and that was why the mothers should have come running after them, leaping down the front steps, flying across the lawn, and begging forgiveness to turn the thing right—so that the children might be the magnanimous ones, the ones in the story who said *yes*.

"Sometimes mothers want to run away, too," I said to my children. It was in the quiet of an aftermath, after a runaway child had been happily delivered into the arms of a cooing mother. I was sitting on the kitchen floor finishing a plate of butterscotch brownies with my own clan, reviewing the events of the past hour, the wailing, the overnight kit, the misunderstanding, the telephone call, the joyful reunion. Our kitchen was suddenly serene and the fun, as so experienced by my two toddlers, was over, although the sweets were not quite gone. I thought to exploit the calm by coasting into a gentle explanation of how everyone in a family needed space and suffered misunderstandings. I was surfing on the soft ocean swells of good feeling, because usually these were the kinds of topics that came on in storms, hurled themselves angrily on the shore, and forced people to shutter up their ears. I knew my children wouldn't understand me. I was just practicing.

"Mama is an aborigine and she is going for a walkabout," I once explained to them as I fled the kitchen taking deep breaths, leaving behind me a squally Past of splattered milk, swatting overtired children, and a sense that if I were queen I should rule better. I toured the house in measured steps, then returned to relative peace, to a mess that availed itself to cleaning. Another time I had tried, "Mama is a Benedictine monk . . ." but it didn't work. My cell was their cell in their eyes.

Hugh was swaying with sleep in the doorway. I picked him up, and he slumped over my shoulder, quietly snoring while I rocked us both, told his dreams that it was snowing, turned on the oven, checked the progress of my thawing blueberries, and then stood at the kitchen door, looking out into the gray dawn of white snow. Past, Present and Future seemed to braid before me, and the snowflakes became a static in the background while I watched memories and dreams separate and bind. Life is a fugue; no strand of melody is abandoned, but it submerges for a time.

I made a bed for Hugh on the living room sofa, though I was loath to give him to it. I could have been a boat grown round a barnacle, so much did I love to carry the warm weight of this child. I spread over him a small blanket I had knit for our firstborn, purling and cabling square after square while the months had plodded to their inexorable end. I kept it downstairs because it belonged to no warm crib. I had folded it neatly on a couch, in a room for adults, and now almost five years later I was unfolding it, over Hugh, as though not only I but my firstborn, too, was ready to give it to him, her little brother. A flush spread through my face and chest, a pleasing sensation that pushed up the corners of my mouth. This was something new. I was used to the old tremors of loss always skulking behind me, as though relegated to prick my heels and curry my spine and chill the nape of my neck. But now, pleasure shivered across the front of me.

Upstairs slept Madeleine, my second daughter, her crib a virtual dry goods store of stuffed animals, toys, and coverlets. I layered squares of cloth over her like some primeval ritual: a thick blanket for warmth, a pink square from the hospital for good luck, a silky cotton shawl for beauty. She kicked them all off during nap or nighttime. She was a firebrand. Only hunger woke her.

The blueberries were ready now, soft, inky, desperate to stain. And there was the snow, outside my window, smothering the earth. I imagined that all things in life had their singular drives— to stain, to smother, to support, to survive, to nurture. The sink said, *Splash me*, and the oven said, *Stuff me*, and the refrigerator, the caretaker, hummed, *I am here, I am here*. I stood in the middle of my kitchen like the clever oiler of their machinery, but a piece of me wished to be elsewhere. A piece of me wanted to walk into the snow, to disappear slowly from view, to draw around myself a watertight line.

I knew the desire to run away was the masked desire to find my own boundaries again, away from the usual traffic of friends and family, that collection of villagers who seemed to have keys of entry and exit to myself. Away from them, I might regain a sense of where my old walls stood and what they circumscribed. But I had a feeling it would amount to an unremarkable kingdom.

I made a simple batter from scratch, because scratch was easier and tasted better than boxes of mixes which promised they were easier and better but tasted worse. I folded the berries into the bumpy buttery-colored slop and they bled their sweet indigo throughout. The oven fan was the sound of heat, a burning coal on this wintry morning. I slid the heavy muffin pan onto a hot rack and ran warm water into the empty batter bowl. So familiar the routine, the feel of my spatula and oven mit, the noise of metal on metal, spoon on clay bowl. There was much to enjoy in being this character in the kitchen, this figure at the hearth, this secret muffin-maker to a household of sleeping bodies. At the same time, part of me was hibernating—waiting for its own spring thaw.

"It is up to you now," I murmured to the oven. Then I turned off the kitchen light, because a winter's dark dawn is best uninterrupted. I blended into the world of snow and sleeping, hushed, like a beating heart hiding from death.

## *Butterscotch Brownies for Runaways*

Oven to 350°

Gently melt:                    2 cups brown sugar
½ cup butter

Let cool slightly.

Add:                            1 cup nuts (optional)
2 eggs                          2 teaspoons baking
2 teaspoons vanilla                powder
1 cup flour                     Salt

Pour into a greased 8 × 8 pan. Bake for 30 to 40 minutes.

Blueberry muffins are a nice touch, but butterscotch brownies are more important in the scheme of things.

⌒

Women rehearse in the kitchen. In those few minutes of down-time, when the muffins are on the road to cresting, when the stew is simmering to solidarity, women relive those things past they might have done differently, and rehearse those things future they would like to do well, because the present is simply engulfed in not letting the muffins incinerate, not letting the stew over-stew. They play out scenes in their minds before letting truth's fingers touch their skin. They may fantasize revenge against the leering washing machine delivery duo; they may fantasize divorce after some painful apparition about their husbands; they may fantasize

Harvard for their progeny. They will be at the kitchen sink, talk-ing to themselves like the nuts on the subway while they cut the spots from fallen apples.

"I have a rich inner life," a friend said to me once, shrugging away the perils to others who became unwitting characters in the staged plays of her mind and then found themselves—through no actual delivery of pernicious lines—demoted, scolded, warned away. Few came out ahead.

I have a rich inner life but I rely on it less. It is faulty until it proves itself otherwise, and I prosecute what it stages for me. It proposes scenarios: Me painting, Me hiking, Me read-ing, Me doing all those things that required hours of the day, but, no Me in the kitchen. I imagine returning from my private larks refreshed, full of the "greetingness of spirit" needed to en-velope children who have been without their always-mother in the kitchen.

I cleared a day, found a sitter, and drove to a museum, thrilling at my own preparedness. I had left the dishes, dirty and clean. I had left the children, clean. I had secured a cargo of quarters for the greedy parking meters. Soon I was down the highway, listen-ing uncomfortably to the loosely clinking belts of the children's car seats. No one counted the exits for me. No little lungs screamed "Bus!!!" at a sighting.

*Nonetheless*, I cheered myself—bagpiper and troop—*there are Stubbs ahead, and Cézannes.* I was determined to have a good time alone, without a stroller or emergency raisins. I made myself beam as I walked along the sidewalk. My antennae, ordinarily trained on the blur of two children in free fall, were picking up exotic signals from a bustling street. I forced myself to look outward, but when I saw a train, when I passed a popsicle vendor, when I bought a bagel, loneliness clapped me on the shoulder. I fantasized about Hugh and Maddie picking out *their* bagels, waving to the diesel engines, just as I fantasized about time alone when I was with them. One day, I reminded myself, the children will leave the house and you had better be ready.

*Ready* was such an immense word. Senta had always tried to warn me. We had to be *ready* for the usual, *ready* for the surprises. I was supposed to *ready* my children for a world of man and nature, neither of which abided by pleasing rules. The smile fell from my face. I was flunking a morning away. I had forgotten how to enjoy myself. I paused at the door to the museum wondering if it was just a B-grade comedy to posit myself in a gallery.

In the ticket line, two women were chatting. They were young and lean and dressed neck to toe in black. They wore huge black shoes that would have served them well on long marches through Normandy. Their mouths were tight red lines. They were Before, and I was After, and for a startling second, I enjoyed being After. *After* had perspective and purpose. I had the impulse to put a maternal arm around these images of perfection and console them. There was something so dogged about their beauty, as though distress had insisted itself in the looming of their look. They seemed unhappy already, and there was so much ahead.

"My brother committed suicide and came back as a crow," one said.

Her friend didn't blink.

*Crows are nice. Some of my best friends are crows*, I thought I would hear.

"That's beautiful," said the friend.

"He sits on my windowsill," said the first woman. She gazed to the side, as though she might find his talons gripping the stair railing; or maybe she had learned to look away when making this avowal, to avoid a meeting glance that registered disbelief, or worse, humor. She had found a place for him, her brother, in the too infinite ethers, so that he could continue to exist for her materially as he did spiritually. We all walked the earth stowing our pains like winter woolens, folding them, patting them, packing them into the scented drawers of our souls, and fingering the knobs in secrecy to assure ourselves that our love had been as astounding as our loss. In this museum hung mournful affirmation—in spades—that sorrow informed us. Here was Judgment Day with its promise of reuniting. Here was a letter dropped to the floor by a hand made limp in sudden anguish.

I glanced at the crow's sister to see if she grasped the testimony on the walls. She and her friend were fixed in front of a Picasso canvas of breasts, buttocks, and eyes—volumes that jutted, sank, and twirled with declaration. Perhaps somewhere inside her a voice whispered, *I, too, have been disassembled and thrust back together in an ugly, unrecognizable, impossibly ambulatory form.*

"Forget it," said her friend. They moved on, but the crow's sister stopped in front of another Cubist canvas. It was a set of clues, as we all are. I kept thinking she was ripe for it, ready to understand its language, because loss was a rogue wave that dashed you on the shoals, and when-and-if you picked yourself up, spit the pebbles from your mouth, retched brine, you would behold the shore differently, as though the whack and deluge had splintered and inked your ways of seeing forever. The crow's sister sighed.

"I wish I could have slept with Picasso," she said.

I hurried from the room into a hall of Tibetan sculpture where my lack of training soothed the sense I couldn't attach to it; it was okay to be inaccessible. *I was a mother of young children*, I glared to a Buddha, and somewhere in between the long nights and the endless needs, my reservoir of casual interest had been supped up. I nearly ran from the museum. I was enlightened. I was refreshed. Now I was desperate to return to my children.

I had stepped out of the realm in which I belonged, then, in those early years of motherhood, when the tedium and sleeplessness just about put you over the precipice, and the distant echo of a husband searching for his once-wife threatens to finish the job, if only because he seeks something to which she has no key herself, yet, something that might sabotage her ability to stay firm for the children when they need her to be as solid and reliable as the earth under their feet. Oil paintings are nice, I found myself humming on the trip home, but offering warm oatmeal to a mouth whose jaw drops open at the sight of a spoon is even nicer. Open Sesame. Now. Not forever. Just now on this detour into motherhood. And I might as well enjoy the scenery, because I won't pass here again, and it is infinitely rich and rewarding.

The trip to the museum was an innocuous experiment with no toxic by-products. When I returned home there were two young children slightly enraged with my thinking that my rich inner life needed expression at the expense of their hold on my simple exterior. I proposed crackers together on the couch, that we might hold on to one another and try to remember it was only three hours ago that I had this look on my face, this look of individuation, this look, like the amnesiac's, that there was something, something, some little thing that existed before.

Motherhood is relentless and it is a miracle that ninety-eight percent of it is tolerable at all. There are emergencies, when a woman suddenly panics that she is drowning in it, losing herself to the blue deep of babies. But it has never been through my children that I met my moments of quiet or raucous desperation, although it has sometimes alarmed me the way I couldn't tolerate the constant prodding of a child. In my house we have all alarmed each other from time to time.

I have called upon my rich inner life often enough, to find metaphors that might lift me from my desire to walk out the door, or whack a child's bottom. I have found images of ocean waves, for instance, that calmed me at first and then proceeded to erode and materially destroy an unoffending beach. I have thought back to the womb, when these children were pushing constantly there, too, as though pushing came long before sucking and suggested that the angels to whom women give birth are only primitive warriors in embryonic form, and that we are merely feeding armies in our kitchens, and these little troops are born to try out their tactics first on us, the mothers, before entering the world of men.

I think of myself as being in the middle of my life, though cancer or accident may prove me wrong. I can no longer find a connection with younger women, and when I see marriage pictures in the newspaper my heart swells with compassion, because my own toddlers have me to protect them for the next decade or so, but these young boys and girls in black and white, cheek to cheek and dizzy smile to dizzy smile, they are on their own now, and it's tough.

They come to my kitchen door around the holidays, young women from a peripheral neighborhood orbit, laden with just-baked cookies and sweet breads, turning up as regularly as a long-basted stitch. They are full of enthusiasm for my children, full of the effervescence of college, with a new need for older women other than their mothers to confide in obliquely. The first time it happened to me I giggled, which was improper behavior, but I had my back turned (she said defensively) and I was giggling not because of the subject matter of young men's desires cloaked in suggestions of English literature, but because I didn't realize how old I'd grown.

I hid my laughter under the plash of water as I washed carrots for a stew. It was wintertime, stew days, and a neighbor's daughter, Lisa, was home for a few weeks of trying her new self out on her mother. Lisa was long and lithe. She did modern dance—no tutu, no toe shoes. She once brought me photographs from a performance in which she wore a brown-and-tan tie-dyed bathing suit and an anguished face. She looked as though she were pushing away a hurricane. Sinews everywhere. In my kitchen, she lounged in a relaxed plie.

How different school holidays looked to student and parent. This young woman had the skin of my young children, the wide smile of someone bursting with secret glory, and the eyes of a no-longer virgin. She arrived bearing fresh brownies wrapped in tin-foil, with a pink ribbon, making me blink because I didn't gift-wrap food any longer, and was it new math or old math that would minimize the gap of years since I did? A friend had asked me recently whether I noticed at parties that men looked past us now and scanned the younger women; but I said—dodging the question so that I could think about it later in private, dragging the idea to my cave so that I could savage it and gnaw the bone in solitude and shamelessness—I said I didn't go to parties anymore, which amounted to the same kind of answer. Yes, I'd noticed. Us—the young mothers not as young as the young heifers who were kicking their heels around the planetary meadow. Heifers that calve become cows; my peers were cows now. The young heifers could find us in our kitchens making wholesome meals that must look hilarious, burlesque, to those who survive on sex and exams and black coffee for months.

But, knock-knock, they came to my door, and danced from toe to toe as they recounted stories they couldn't tell their mothers. *I miss so-and-so like crazy!* The truth is, no so-and-so lasts long, and This Is Not Advice but: You do not have to remember his name, because they stack up as quickly as airplanes waiting for takeoff. These women wanted out of the dormitory, they told me, needed an apartment of their own, with a kitchen, so that they could make cookies for the queue of hims, who in the sixties my mother referred to as woolly mammoths for their terror of personal hygiene, who in the nineties looked to me more like aimless wannabes, too cynical to find a mentor or hero anywhere—all simply college boys, trembling with sexual energy and living side-by-side with young women with rucksacks full of books without pictures.

"It's a question of gender," Lisa said, apropos of practically nothing.

"Not at your age," I fired back. "At your age it's a question of sex."

She giggled. She knew we could talk.

"Who said that sex is wasted on the young?" I grumbled, feeling o-l-d.

More giggles. It didn't feel wasted.

I pulled a sack of frozen corn from the freezer while Lisa regaled me with the romance of the new Him. My mother said fresh corn was wasted in stews. She said you could use frozen corn, frozen peas, even frozen pearl onions if your stew base was tasty enough, by which she meant good meat and better red wine. My mother preferred to tell me about frozen vegetables when I would come home from college and wander into the kitchen with a look in my eye that said *boy-stuff*. She wrote in her books that you were old enough to sleep with a man when you didn't have to tell your mother. Ah-hem.

Hence the mother next door. I was not as old as Lisa's mother and so I might—*might*—still understand; and it was clear that any line of consternation which dared to wiggle across my forehead would trigger a massive shut-down, Lisa having only just washed herself of the messy finger paints of adolescence, and still in the habit of raising the castle drawbridge up from the moat when she saw anything remotely threatening to the order of her new kingdom.

Was it possible that I was on the mothery sensible side of this conversation? The situation was terribly funny to me, for which I patted myself on the back: Good for you for finding humor in this moment of locating yourself on the other side of the hill when you didn't realize you had crested and begun the descent.

Good for you for not mentioning the morning in your early thir-ties when you woke up to spider veins, cysts that needed removal, the weakening of unmentionables. Good for you for not leaking the news that woolly mammoths weren't cute in their thirties, and that husbands veered off when the children came, and you were left to find some way to become a good friend to a mate growing tangentially to yourself. Good for you for not using that needle, with which Lisa was basting herself into the fat quilty bunting of my own square life, to pierce her balloon.

There I was, aproned not because I was making this grand-motherly stew but because my children were painting on news-paper on the kitchen floor and they needed something on which to clean their hands and brushes in between colors. I was an old swatchy Clyfford Still canvas, surveyed by young eyes and found safe, which is trouncing to the spirit, and which should be a warning to Clyfford Still that he might be patted on the head in the future after a lifetime of being regarded as a renegade.

I was making stew because I thought it was the right thing to do in winter, as though some convention of Western matrons had voted it Article 5, Paragraph B, under the heading of De-cember. I was making house, as my mother instructed. The child labor laws prohibited me from thrusting the responsibility onto any toddler who couldn't reach the stovetop knobs.

And here is my recipe for stew, a minute's rest from Lisa and her bed:

## Basic Stew

1 package of lamb
  or beef cut up for
  stew, about 1½
  pounds
Olive oil for sauté
2 onions, chopped
  (a few shallots are
  better)
3 carrots, chopped
Several bay leaves—
  don't stint
1 open bottle of red
  wine, too old to
  drink, but not bad;
  you'll need 2 cups

1 cup frozen peas
1 cup frozen corn
However many pearl
  onions you can
  stand to peel or
  about a cup of
  frozen pearl onions
1 large can crushed
  tomatoes
1 tablespoon grated
  lemon zest
Fistful of peppercorns
Thyme
Sage
Salt and pepper

Flop the meat pieces in flour. In a big pot, sear the meat in olive oil, then set it aside on a dish. Use that flavored oil, plus some extra, to brown the chopped onions. Onions taste best when slightly burnt, so keep the heat higher than usual and don't abandon them. Throw in the carrots, the seasoning, a cup of wine, and the bouillon. After a few minutes, put the meat back in. Add some more wine. After half an hour, throw in the rest of the vegetables and let the whole thing simmer for an hour, or until the meat is tender, tender.

Toss in the lemon zest and cook for another 10 minutes.

Pick out the bay leaves.

Serve over a bed of fat noodles prepared with butter and caraway seeds.


Lisa was watching me cook with total disinterest, her eyes telescoping inward to memories of the wannabe and his heroic morality, the two of them struggling with the tragedy of Christmas that had separated them for the holidays, although likely it would be a different wannabe from whom she would be separated on tragic Easter, the two of them thinking they were atoms separated by space but linked by the mysterious quantum theory of the heart, working out the abc's of being civil to one another, and exploitative at the same time, albeit under independent roofs. Was he at his home, sighing about his princess, eating soup among brothers? He was probably off skiing, thinking of moguls and hot chocolate and skinny females in tight ski pants. Not because he didn't love Lisa to the end of his synapses—nay—but because his synapses were a little shorter than in the movie.

"Will you stay for stew?" I invited, when the stew was set to simmer and I had cleaned up a colorful paella of newsprint and wet paint from the kitchen floor. It was a safe proposition. Young women don't eat stew because it smells to them of older women and larger waistlines. I imagined I could convince a nine-year-old to eat my stew by arguing it was only thick soup; then there would be a hiatus until the child was in its mid-twenties and I could say, "This isn't stew, it's cassoulet," using a soft French accent to heighten the appeal, and having subtracted out the beans and duck confit I would serve it with flat noodles, and it would become incarnations of cassoulet until the child hit its mid-thirties, when the constricting skin of youth would have finally molted and fallen into the gully reeds, drying to dust, and the child, now a parent, would be free to experience simple things again with simple pleasure.

Lisa admitted she couldn't join us for stew. She stretched, awkwardly, thinking she should make her exit, not wanting to go yet. "Did my mom mention the off-campus apartment?"

"No," I said, suddenly feeling sorry for her mother.

"It would be so much less expensive than a dorm room," Lisa chirped, prom queen of cost-cutting.

I smiled thoughtfully at Lisa, who liked to drag her mattress into my kitchen. "I don't want to minimize your experience," I said carefully to her. "But I hope a more peaceful decade awaits you." That is what my mother used to say to her daughters, one after another, as we rode out our early independence like bronco busters at the rodeo.

My mother wrote a book once about a young woman she called a born-again virgin. She knew there often comes a time when young women want to start over, because the basic recipe for sex—the, say, *Joy of Cooking* recipe for sex—is too easy, and they want to try another recipe, one that includes a cup of meaning. Because there is something besides Darwin, beyond the desire to send a million parachuted seeds into the wind that draws human beings together; we have the chance to let love grow the way a child grows—from wonderfully untamed to wonderfully earnest.

I pulled a big pasta pot from a lower cupboard. Broad, flat noodles with butter, salt, and caraway seeds are excellent with stew or brisket. My mother loved them. She called them never-fail noodles. I thought to tell Lisa, but when I looked up, it startled me to see her eyes brimming with tears. She gave a snort unbecoming a geisha and put her face in her hands. All those smiles, pliés, and brownies in pink ribbons—they burned like matches, quick and bright.

"It's so tumultuous," she stammered. "And it's not"—she burst into tears—"love."

"No," I said, and put my arms around her. Lisa's world, which had seemed so foolproof when she walked into my kitchen, now seemed riddled with folly. It might have been a staggering elucidation were it not Lisa-in-College; she would be fine in the morning.

Suddenly we felt our knees and thighs clasped, and we looked down to find Hugh and Maddie hugging our legs. It was very moving—the sight of these two young children so unafraid of grown-up tears. They were great comforters, big back-patters when they could reach.

"Now you feel better," Hugh said to Lisa, showing her a big how-to smile. Then he handed her a toy.

⌒

"But there's no place to sit," my mother would despair, *in certain museums*, she might say, *that shall go nameless*. This was her way to shame all nouns, all persons, places, and things that weren't keeping up their end of the social contract. They would go nameless, they would know who they were, they would hear her allusion, and they might improve themselves under the naked whip of her clothed reproach.

Those were the days, I want to tell her, when you could hu-
miliate someone. Nowadays, people are shameless, vote into office shameless presidents, remarry shameless men, raise shameless
children. You're missing a great moment in degeneracy, Mama.

The news would get her down for half a day, the morning
hours, until noon and toast with cottage cheese and the promise
of an afternoon dawning with clean aspirations. It was a short
time to process bad news about life on earth, one morning, within
the context of eternity.

For me, the mornings can drag their heels in the vast pale
dunes of seconds and minutes and hours, when of course the
children won't eat what they're served, throw up what goes down,
stand mesmerized and queasy at the open refrigerator door while
I, tethered in the middle of the kitchen, clean up, hug, scream
(*shut the refrigerator door!*), hug, serve (*maybe a pretzel?*), wash.
These are lonely mornings in which the images of Greek kouroi
and the madness of Gogol jeer at me like gargoyles, dare me to
transport my thoughts to a higher plateau, but I can't, because I
have to comfort two lurching, moaning, sick, and hungry children, and because I am hopelessly caught in the earthy maelstrom
of my first midlife crisis, my premenopausal midlife crisis, the
Grand Pivot when the woman is done with childbearing and must
enter the second half of her life in which child rearing and regaining her identity are like two horses in a neck-and-neck race.
Eventually it's wise to put good money on the regaining of the
self and hope that the children don't end up in jail. I yearn for
my mother now, to chart part two.

"Again you're gone," I say to the air that is scented with vomit
and coffee. But I have said it dispassionately this time, as though

the sword blade were no longer twisting in my belly. True, she is not there with a cold wet washcloth to fold and press on a small hot forehead. But she is there, and how convenient that she doesn't need a chair. She knelt in the grasses of cemeteries, spread blankets in churchyards, found comfortable slices of battered rock at Segesta. She will make do in my kitchen, and I must make do with that certainty. In fact, I know she can't tear herself away; she is captivated by my two queasy children.

"*I can feel my tubes untying,*" she used to murmur when she saw babies.

You have lots of grandchildren, I could tell her now. Dad is teaching them all how to play poker, turning his new house into a cheery version of the war trench. I gave you one to cradle in your lap, to rock until I get there. But I'm done having them, Mama. The cells in my body are calling for a moratorium on division and replication. My children are now on the earth, or in it, or above it perhaps, but no longer waiting to be conceived. My eggs have had their day as pollen does, and queen bees do, and now I have to redefine myself for the next few decades that are so un-Darwinian, that want me not at all unless I devise a reason to exist here, that have no design or purpose unless I create one.

You once wrote that it was really when the offspring left the nest that the mother might reemerge, although that wasn't what you did; you couldn't wait that long, but dove into your self while I was still a child, so deft you were at managing children by then, so sure that going back to work was a good model for your little girls. I felt all my life that I glided into the world in the breeze of your relief that you could finally have your tubes tied.

243

It was the Guttmacher Formula in those days that stipulated guidelines for women who should be allowed a tubal ligation: five children at thirty-five, six children at thirty. You had five at thirty-six, became the first woman to have the surgery in Northampton. The Catholic nurses were allowed to leave the operating room, and that was that. You did it, and you recorded it to me as a moment of profound deliverance, a stone set in front of the cave entrance, leaving pregnancies behind and releasing you for the future of open air. I grew up linked to that moment when you would bear no more, feeling like one who had squeaked under the limbo stick. Your tubal ligation cemented me in life as the last child, the baby of the family, defined me critically and incontrovertibly. My birth and the end of your bearing children—a hazy association and it haunts me now as I ponder the demolition of my own fallopian tubes, blasting the tendril highway so that no new troops can march down it.

But up comes the pretzel with a plash, and a sob, and I wonder why I thought it would stay down, and I wish someone were here to hold the shaking little body while I cleaned the floor. Then I glance up, and I see the rectangular shape of this child's woeful mouth, the shape of a heavy mattress carried on a head, a crescented rectangle, waaaah. It is transporting, this image of a small misery. I wrap my arms around the bundle of warm wailing and enjoy being the mother who can soothe and sing away the spasms of a belly. There will be so much in their lives that I will not be able to solve, so many awful times when all I will be able to do is acknowledge, hold a hand, try to explain why I introduced them to a world of suffering; and so I fall out of my own preoccupations and into the open greedy maw of mothering, and I keep my arms tight around the tiny creature whose heavy head is beginning to resonate with snores, and I lift him up, out of the kitchen, upstairs to his bed to sleep past the breakfast that wouldn't sit.

Then it is back to the kitchen, to my daughter on the floor with a book about a fish. I sigh, and slump down next to her, my back against a cupboard full of pots. I am feeling like a cupboard full of eggs. I have lost my self for years in the automatic march of life, and I reach, lunge, for remembrance, as though memories were the Braille of self-revelation. I am one of the few things I have lost that I may find again. My mother is gone, and my first baby girl is gone, and I survive those losses in the echoes of my love; and though I look inside to find them, it is only me I'm bumping up against, and what about me reflects their absences. The presences, then, of two children in my kitchen swell up against the pain; and the two, absence and presence, seem to stare at each other with wonder, like Narcissus and his reflection in the pool of water, staring, sensing kinship, raising an eyebrow, saying nothing. My two breathing children will grow up staring into the empty air to find their grandmother and their sister. They will track down what shaped them that they did not know, and it will be those two absences, vast and beautiful, that shaped their mother, who shaped them.

I am destined to work out this stage change in my kitchen. It has always been that way, from the first steps to the first words, from the hum of my mother among her friends and children to the hum of myself among my friends and children—it is there in the kitchen that the remarkable moments occur; the kitchen, like a renewable cocoon from which I continue to emerge, phase after phase.

Now as a young mother, inexplicably stuck to a cupboard door, I find peace. My kitchen is alive. I am wrapped there by the resounding life of my children. They love this kitchen for its cell-like chambers filled with things that go clang, crash, *fthlink, fthlunk*. They love the way it is clean every morning, waiting for them to extract and disassemble. They think there is no better place for trains to chug and stuffed animals to share raisins. They thrive on the trill of danger, creeping up to my heels and wondering if I know they're there. What brilliance, they feel, using the overturned salad bowl to reach new things, like knives. My children are the drivers of Apollo's chariot; they pull me up into the bright sky, away from my earthly sorrows.

I look beside me to this small girlchild with her finger on the picture of a luminous fish, and I can almost hear her brother snoring in his bed, and I can almost feel her grandmother and her shadow sister; and I imagine myself reaching further to touch my sisters, my brother, my father, my friends. We are all here together, the sleeping and the dead, the born and the unborn, here in the cells that construct us, here in the alchemy of our souls, here in the kitchen of juice and cracker, wine and bread, blood and flesh.

# ACKNOWLEDGMENTS

Encouragement is a love song, but the list of all those who have encouraged me reads like a simple chant. Thank you, Kathy Anderson, agent, friend, foil, editor, ear. Thank you, Fran Kamin, for letting me, and Helene Rabinovitz, for making me. Thank you, Diane Higgins, Rebecca Wilson, Jane Bradish-Ellames, and Patricia Fernandez for your enthusiasm and ideas. Thank you, Paul, Tony, Julia, Maggie, and Jennifer, standing like tall pines in the meadow of my mind. Thanks to my wonderful book group—go easy on me, please. Thank you, Hugh and Madeleine, expanding daily the boundaries of my love. And of course there would be nothing without Chuck Zabriskie, the trellis on which I climb. We remember you, Elizabeth, the soil ever fresh above your head. Take care of her, Mama, my muse.